The Vegan Survival Guide

*How to Eat a Plant-Based Diet and Live
Compassionately without Losing Your
Friends and Social Life*

Victoria Simmons

that the author is not engaging in the rendering of legal, financial, medical or professional advice. The content within this book has been derived from various sources. Please consult a licensed professional before attempting any health choices outlined in this book.

By reading this document, the reader agrees that under no circumstances is the author responsible for any losses, direct or indirect, which are incurred as a result of the use of information contained within this document, including, but not limited to, — errors, omissions, or inaccuracies.

Table of Contents

Don't Turn Down Invitations Just Because You're Vegan

Be Prepared
Let Them Know
Don't Take it Personally
Have an Open Mind

Chapter 5: It's Your Birthday? Throw an Epic Vegan Birthday Party!

NOW It's All About You!

Set the Rules
Drinks
Cake
Games and Activities
Avoid Preachiness or Imposition of Your Vegan Lifestyle on Your Guests

Chapter 6: Meal Prep

Why It's Important

How to Plan Your Meals
How Not to Waste
Meal Prep on a Budget

Chapter 7: Limiting Beliefs

The Most Frustrating Beliefs About the Vegan Lifestyle

#1 - "I'll have to eat boring food like salads without flavor for the rest of my life!"
#2 - "I can't give up cheese."
#3 - "I am actively doing sports, and I need animal protein."
#4 - "I'll have to take a bunch of supplements and vitamins."
#5 - "People will think of me as a weirdo and even my family wouldn't support me."

Introduction

Welcome to the vegan survival guide! Since you're reading this particular book, I'm assuming that you're vegan, you've just begun the vegan lifestyle, or you're thinking about becoming a vegan (which, by the end of this book, I hope you'll decide to go for!). As a vegan myself, I'd like to thank and congratulate you for your wonderful lifestyle choice. By going vegan, you're choosing to stay healthy without having to cause harm to our planet, to innocent animals and to yourself.

However, if you're looking for a preachy, pushy book, this isn't it! Here, I'll try to help you survive your vegan journey which I know for a fact, isn't going to be easy. Hopefully, through this book, you won't take this new part of your life too seriously. The more positive thoughts you have, the more successful you will be, trust me. Of course, becoming a true vegan is a process, and it doesn't happen overnight. In fact, for a lot of people, it takes a long time, especially for those who aren't really sure about their decision. The important thing is to take all the time you need to adjust, learn, and finally, accept that you're a vegan by choice.

As you begin your vegan journey, prepare yourself to deal with different types of people. Some people try their best to convince you that this is a wrong decision, others will feel dubious and start questioning you about your choice, and, if you're lucky, some people will also support you every step of the way even if they're not vegan themselves. No matter what type of people you encounter during your journey, this book will hopefully empower you with the methods and skills you need to keep yourself motivated, survive social interactions and gatherings, and talk to different people about veganism in a polite, positive, and enlightening way.

In times when you're having trouble sticking with your lifestyle choice, you will need all the help you can get! Even at the start of my own journey, I had to look for motivation from different sources. From people to online resources, written resources, and more, I had to go through a lot to maintain my stance. This is one of the main reasons why I wrote this book in the first place. Since I was lucky enough to overcome all those challenges, I want to help you and every other unsure vegan-to-be out there.

As you go through the different chapters of this book, you'll learn how to face challenges head-on, remain motivated, and banish any doubts you have about veganism. If you've started following the vegan diet and you're finding it extremely difficult because almost everyone around you is non-vegan, you're not alone! We've all been there, and I will be the first to admit that it can be tough. But with the right information, tips, tricks, and methods, you will be able to survive your vegan journey without feeling hurt or without hurting or offending those around you. So... shall we begin?

Chapter 1
Why Do People Fail on a Vegan Diet?

Nowadays, more and more people are choosing to become vegan. Just like me, most of these people believe that the vegan diet is the most beneficial and natural diet human beings can follow. Of course, I also know that not everybody accepts this belief and that's okay. But for all the vegans out there, do you know why some people fail when they try to follow a vegan lifestyle?

Before we go into the most common reasons why people fail on this diet, let's establish this first: this book is NOT a holier-than-thou book about veganism. I didn't start off as a vegan; I merely adopted the lifestyle when I learned more about it. And so I'm sharing all of this information with you to help you deal with this lifestyle choice which, let's face it, can sometimes be quite challenging.

So let's go back to the topic at hand. Why do people fail on a vegan diet? Although there are many reasons, let's take a look at the most common.

The Vegan Diet Can Be Challenging

Although thinking about following the vegan diet isn't uncommon, the diet itself isn't so easy to follow. It's something many people think about starting, especially when they're in the self-exploration phase. But once some people start the diet and have stuck with it for some time, they realize that it's too much of a lifestyle change for them.

One main reason for this is that a lot of people don't find the vegan diet to be convenient. Although more and more establishments are providing vegan options for us (kudos to them, by the way), finding vegan-friendly food items isn't as easy as finding non-vegan foods. Another reason a lot of people get intimidated with the vegan diet is that they don't have the necessary kitchen skills. In other words, they can't cook, and cooking is an important part of veganism, especially if you're on a budget and you want to make sure that everything, you're eating is purely vegan.

These are the main reasons why people don't follow through with the vegan diet. Let's look at the other common reasons for this.

Reason #1 - Lack of Support

Unfortunately, veganism has gained a negative reputation, especially in mainstream America. When some people hear somebody, they know say "I'm vegan," they raise their eyebrows immediately. For a few lucky ones, the people around them support them from the very start and even encourage their new lifestyle choice.

But just like the majority of people who have chosen to go vegan, I've also experienced a lack of support from my family. And this is one of the main reasons why a lot of people fail on a vegan diet too. Speaking from experience, trying to begin a whole new lifestyle without the support of your loved ones is *tough*!

The sad truth is, though, I was also guilty of being a negative Nancy when it came to veganism in the past. I also used to see vegans as self-righteous, snotty people who just wanted to push their beliefs on others. I got that image of vegans from... surprise, surprise! My family. Of course, the media and other people around me didn't help at all. Veganism has a bad reputation because that's what the general public thinks (but I still hope that things will change soon).

But when I tried to learn more about going vegan, it was then when I actually understood what it was all about. The more I learned about veganism, the more I wanted to start adopting the lifestyle. Sure, I got a lot of sermons and questions from my family and friends, but I stuck with my decision. And when I was confident enough about everything, I learned about being a vegan, I shared my reasons with my loved ones. Tough as it was, I talked to them about what I had learned about veganism and why I decided to become a vegan.

Yes, I had to deal with a few eye rolls from some of my

friends, but the more I enlightened them, the more they understood me. Of course, I didn't push my lifestyle or try to impose it upon them; I merely shared my own reasons for choosing to become a vegan. It took some time, but I've not become one of the lucky ones because my friends and family now support me! So, if you're stuck in a rut and you feel like giving up because of the lack of support, don't give up just yet.

Talk to your support system about your choice and try to make them understand why you took this path. If they need time to accept the "new you," then give them the time. In the meantime, there are other places where you can get support from such as online forums, support groups, and whatnot which can help you appreciate the vegan lifestyle more and help you stick with your decision to go vegan.

Reason #2 - Refusing to Face the Truth

This is another important reason why a lot of people fail on a vegan diet. You've probably heard that old adage "the truth hurts." As a lover of learning, this part didn't really hinder me from becoming a vegan. But for a lot of people, they don't WANT to face the truth. Instead of learning why choosing the vegan lifestyle is a good option, most people prefer to continue eating whatever they want without thinking about the consequences.

Part of adopting the vegan lifestyle is learning *why* this

lifestyle might be the better choice. This means that you may have to watch some documentaries which show animal abuse and, trust me; those images can never be unseen. But if you find the courage to face the truth about how they treat the animals in slaughterhouses and in farms, this will make it easier for you to accept veganism. These documentaries exist to make you aware of the torture being done to the animals and the pain they feel, just so we can eat the food we grew up loving.

So, if you're thinking about becoming a vegan or if you've already started, but you're having a hard time following through, maybe it's time for you to face the truth. As another popular adage goes, "the truth shall set you free!" Becoming a vegan is a choice, and part of that choice is to learn the reasons behind the lifestyle and to accept them in order to embrace this huge change in your life.

It's particularly hard for people who want to start this lifestyle to take this step. Think about it, you've been eating meat all your life, and suddenly, you find out the truth about how your food choices affect other living things! It's scary, tough to absorb, and even tougher to accept. It's tough, but not impossible. As long as you keep an open mind, the whole transition process will become a whole lot easier.

Reason #3 - Not Eating Enough Calories

One of the reasons you may have wanted to become a vegan is that you want to eat healthier foods. But when you eliminate meat and dairy products from your diet, it can sometimes feel like there's nothing left for you to eat! We've all been there, especially at the beginning of our transition. I myself have experienced going to the local supermarket feeling highly motivated only to look at the shelves and realize that I cannot actually eat the majority of food items they offer. For some people, this can be a huge turn off which, in turn, causes them to give up the vegan lifestyle altogether.

But the truth is, there are plenty of food choices for vegans, and if you choose the right foods, you won't have to worry that you're not eating enough calories each day. Really, veganism isn't about starving yourself. Otherwise, nobody would choose this lifestyle at all! Of course, it's true that some people choose to go vegan in order to lose weight. But just because these people actually shed pounds after going vegan, this isn't true for all of us. Basically, it all comes down to your food choices.

While you're on a vegan diet, you must make sure that you're getting enough calories each day. Of course, if you lower your food choices to raw foods, as some vegans do, you risk ripping yourself off nutrients, which eventually can weaken your immune system. When eating a plant-based diet, it's notoriously important to always monitor your macronutrients. All vegans (and not only) need to make sure their diet is balanced, and that it includes carbohydrates, protein, fats, water, fiber, vitamins and minerals. In terms of nutrition, the diet makes a lot of sense since you can keep on eating all those nutritious whole foods which means that you won't end up being deficient in a particular nutrient... that is, as I said, IF you eat a balanced diet and you always make yourself aware of what you're eating.

A lot of people believe that vegans aren't getting all the nutrients they need because of all the food items they've removed from their diets. But in reality, we can still get those valuable nutrients just from different sources. So it's all about finding the right food items and the proper portions to be sufficiently nourished every day.

Reason #4 - Too Much Junk Food

Okay, for some people, going vegan means that they eat a lot of junk foods which are "vegan-friendly" and "mock meats" which are actually processed and thus, not good for the health. If you're one of these people who has started the vegan lifestyle only to choose unhealthy options such as these, chances are, you won't feel too good, and you might end up gaining a lot of weight. Unfortunately, when this happens, a lot of people feel frustrated, demotivated, and would start thinking that the vegan lifestyle is a sham!

It's sad, really.

So we go back to educating yourself about the vegan diet or lifestyle. If you really want to stick to a plant-based diet, do it properly! Since the vegan diet has gained some popularity recently, food manufacturers have taken advantage of this trend. They've created "vegan-friendly" products which are processed and not at all healthy. But if you really follow the vegan diet, you should focus on plant-based food items which are healthy and which will provide you with the health benefits you're looking for.

No matter what type of diet you choose to follow, if you opt for the junk foods which are supposedly okay for that diet, you won't be seeing the positive results you're looking for-- those who motivated you to start following the diet in the first place. What I'm trying to say is that if you want to love how you feel and look in your body, make sure to find the balance. I'm not saying that you have to be too hard on yourself. That won't work either. But what I am saying is that you should be smart when it comes to choosing the foods you will eat each day. Maybe you want to experiment in the kitchen and surprise your guests with vegan pizza, lasagna, burgers or hotdogs – then go for the mock meats. But if your everyday-menu consists mainly of those, odds are you won't stick to this lifestyle long. It will be to hard on your metabolism, you might gain weight and you will end up spending fortune on those vegan treats.

Based on experience, the health benefits of the vegan diet are plenty. You'll start feeling better about your health and the more challenges you overcome, the easier it will be for you to follow this lifestyle. So ditch the junk, read the labels, and do your research on the proper food items you should be eating. When reading food labels, stay away from GMOs, textured proteins, hydrolyzed proteins, and other strange-sounding ingredients. Even if the product claims that it's vegan, if it contains any ingredients which you don't understand, put it down and search for something else. As much as possible, opt for whole foods instead of junk foods. This will help reduce the likelihood of you failing on the vegan diet!

Reason #5 - Budget

Last, but definitely not least, is the budget. A lot of people believe that following a vegan lifestyle will break the bank. Just like the other diet trends which have emerged in the past few years, when people think about the vegan diet (which is new to them), they can already imagine their wallets getting emptied.

This is one of the common misconceptions about the vegan diet. Think about it; don't meat products, eggs, and dairy products cost a lot more than vegan-friendly food items such as rice, lentils, beans, potatoes, bananas, and others? If you choose these whole foods, you'll actually save a lot of money in the long run! Of course, you should skip those fancy "vegan" food items which do cost a lot but, as we've talked about in the last point, aren't actually healthy.

If you do your research about which foods you can eat when choosing this lifestyle, you'll come to realize that they're actually more affordable! Don't start following the vegan lifestyle with the mindset that you're about to start an expensive endeavor. Doing this will surely ensure your failure. Instead, think about how much you'll save because you won't have to spend money on dairy products, eggs, meat products, and other costly food items which contain them.

And if you have cooking skills (which I didn't have at the beginning of my vegan journey), all the better! You will be able to whip up some amazing meals using fresh but cheap ingredients. If you don't have cooking skills, don't fret. I started out with zero cooking skills too. But now, I can actually cook some pretty tasty dishes thanks to all of the available resources online such as recipes for vegan fares.

If you don't have any cooking skills, make this a part of your journey. Trust me, learning how to cook is both enjoyable and satisfying. And when you're able to cook your own meals, you'll realize how fulfilling it is. Also, you won't have to purchase vegan dishes from restaurants and food establishments which, strangely enough, come at higher prices. Eventually, you'll discover how economical the vegan lifestyle is, and this can be a huge motivator for you.

So, get rid of your belief that you don't have the budget for a vegan lifestyle and start focusing on the positive aspects of the diet!

Chapter 2:
Eating Vegan on the Road

Being on the road can be both exhilarating and stressful for anyone. First, there are the happy feelings you have, the excitement of seeing new places, having new experiences, and meeting new people can almost make you forget that you're a vegan.

Almost.

Then you start wondering about what you're going to eat while on the road when most roadside restaurants and food establishments don't offer vegan-friendly fare. Even though you've already established a good routine at home, and you've become familiar with the local restaurants which have vegan dishes, you might not be able to follow your diet properly while you're on the road. That is unless you prep all of your meals for the whole trip from day one to the last day. But depending on how long your trip is or how frequently you plan to travel, this might mean preparing and packing a WHOLE lot of food to bring with you.

Sadly, traveling is another aspect which is quite difficult for vegans, especially at the beginning or when you're traveling to a place which you know is famous for meat dishes and other non-vegan fares. Of course, these reasons shouldn't stop you from traveling. Just like any other challenge, this one comes with a solution. You don't have to give up veganism while you're traveling nor do you have to give up traveling just to maintain your vegan lifestyle. It's all about planning, researching, and strategizing if you want to have your vegan cake and eat it too!

In this chapter, we'll be talking about how to remain vegan while traveling. By learning some clever tips and tricks, you won't have to worry about traveling or staying on the road for a long time, even when you're traveling with your non-vegan friends and family. Then you'll come to realize how enriching the vegan lifestyle is because you'll get to explore other dishes and plant-based options from the places you visit.

The Most Difficult Challenge

If you've ever tried going on a trip as a vegan without preparing for it first, you may have had a very difficult experience. If you haven't tried this yet, let me share my own experience with you. The first time I went on a trip with my friends a couple of months after I've made the choice to follow the vegan path, I only realized that I didn't prepare for the trip when we stopped over to eat.

Of course, the diner we went into didn't have any vegan food options. All they had were burgers, hot dogs and sandwiches, and nothing that I can eat. So there I sat with my friends wanting to cry because I was so hungry and they all ordered foods which I used to love. Of course, I was frustrated. But I tried my best to shut out all the sights and smells while still trying to keep up my end of the conversation.

Was it difficult? YES! But the good thing was that my friends did show their support to me. They kept asking me if it was okay for them to eat when I couldn't order anything from the menu. They also kept apologizing to me for picking that particular diner. Although my stomach was grumbling, I appreciated their words and sentiments, so I simply nodded, smiled, and told them that I wasn't so hungry.

That experience was both good and bad for me. It made me realize that I need to prepare myself before going on a trip if I didn't want to starve from start to finish. And it was because of that trip that I had learned to research, and plan before going on any adventure. If you're wondering if I didn't eat anything for the whole trip, don't worry. My friends and I were able to find a grocer which offered a lot of vegan food items, and I stocked up nuts, fruits, plant-based yoghurt and fresh buns! So all in all, I had a happy ending.

Tips for Remaining Vegan While Traveling

As I've said, just because you've started following the vegan lifestyle, this doesn't mean that you're done with traveling. However, this sometimes means that eating while traveling won't always be an easy and glamorous experience (of course, if you're always able to see the good in the situation, you don't have to worry that much). If you really plan to stick with your diet, there are times when you will have to eat meals which are unexciting or bland compared to the dishes enjoyed by your friends and loved ones. Although some places do offer amazing vegan dishes, you might experience more challenges than victories. But follow these tips, and you'll surely make your travels easier and more fun.

1. **Do your research**

   The first and most important step in your preparation and planning is to do your research. Learn all about the place you're going to before you actually go. That way, you can determine whether or not you'll be able to find vegan-friendly food in your destination. Think about it, when you plan vacations, you do some research about these places anyway. You learn about the best spots to visit, the best places to stay, the best things to do, and the best places to eat. So including the vegan options into your research won't be that hard at all.

   Apart from learning more about the place you'll be going to, you may also want to learn a couple of basic phrases in the local dialect of your destination.

This allows you to show your interest and respect to the locals and it also allows you to ask about the food that's being served to you. Apart from the basic greetings, you may also want to learn how to say "I am vegan" in the local language so you can say this to your servers at the local restaurants. If your server understands you and offers you a vegan-friendly menu, you just overcame a huge hurdle! And you'll be able to enjoy a delicious meal that's specially meant for your lifestyle. It's definitely a win-win situation.

If you have a LOT of time to do research, you may even learn the local terms for meat, eggs, and dairy products. That way, you can look at the descriptions of the dishes on menus and determine if they contain any of the food items which you aren't allowed to eat.

2. Learn about the culture of your destination

As part of your research, learn more about the roots of veganism in your destination. This will help you understand how the locals might respond or react to you telling them that you're a vegan. Remember, there's a big difference between you telling a server that you're a vegan and asking your server if the vegan dish on the menu contains any dairy products, meat products, eggs or any other type of food you're not allowed to eat.

Also, you may want to find out if the place you're going to has any vegan organizations. There may be groups in the area who get together to host potlucks or to celebrate in restaurants with other vegans. If you do find any of these places or events, it would be a lot of fun to join in! I myself have yet to experience this since I've always traveled on days when such events weren't scheduled. But I'd sure want to try!

3. Learn about the food items in the place you're going to

Think about the types of food you'd like to eat while on your trip. For instance, if you love vegan bread, learn about the specialty bread products of your destination. Some types of bread require eggs and milk so you should stay away from these.

Or if you're in a restaurant which doesn't offer any vegan dishes, take a look at the sides. There may be a lot of options and ordering a couple of these sides can comprise an entire meal already!

Then there are the local markets. As part of your tour, why not drop by one of the local markets in your destination? As soon as you check-in to your accommodation, ask the locals about the nearest markets or grocery stores in the area. It's always fun to go through the aisles and discover local food items which are both delicious and vegan-friendly!

If you're traveling to a different country and the local cuisine is completely non-vegan, you can search for international options. Usually, Indonesian, Thai, Indian, and other Asian or Mediterranean places offer vegan-friendly dishes.

Apart from learning about the food items, you also have the option to call the restaurants in your destination ahead of time. Of course, this requires a lot more time and effort from you, but it will be worth it. I've tried this a couple of times during my travels, and I've always had amazing conversations with the people I've spoken to. Then whenever I arrived at these restaurants, I've been greeted by the ones I've talked to on the phone with warmth as if I was an honored guest. It's really quite nice.

4. Pack a lot of tasty and filling snacks for your trip

This is one of the most practical tips I can ever share with you. Try searching for tips online for eating vegan while traveling and you'll always see this tip. Although you don't have to prepare all of your daily meals for the trip, packing a bunch of tasty and filling snacks will go a long way.

Keep these snacks with you on-hand so that you can munch on them while on the road, while walking strolling around the streets, while on your flight, or even while you're in the hotel. Sometimes, these snacks will also come in handy when you aren't able to find any restaurants or establishments which offer vegan-friendly fares.

Just make sure that the snacks you bring are healthy, filling, easy to transport, and don't spoil easily, especially if you're planning to be on the road for a long time. Also, snacks which are easy to eat are the best, so you won't have to worry about leaving a mess wherever you go. Some of my favorite snacks to bring are fruits, nuts, trail mix, granola, protein bars, and even roasted chickpeas. If you have your own favorite snacks, bring them along with you!

5. Choose an accommodation which has a kitchen so that you have the option to cook

If you want to be able to eat everything you want on your trip or you don't want to deviate too much from your usual diet, you may want to choose an accommodation which comes with a kitchen. That way, you have the option to cook your meals after getting fresh ingredients from the local groceries or farmer's markets.

Knowing that you have the option to cook will make you feel more excited about your trip. Back when I didn't know how to cook (one skill which I only learned when I became a vegan), I only looked forward to eating my favorite snacks or finding some great restaurants which offer vegan dishes.

But since learning how to cook vegan dishes, I always make sure to choose hotels, apartments or units which have kitchens of their own. Then I make it a point to take a trip to the local markets to find some fresh and unique ingredients to make some awesome dishes. In fact, I've gotten pretty good at experimenting that my friends and family even look forward to the dishes I whip up!

6. Always be a good guest by remaining polite and flexible

Before you travel, make sure to tell your companions that you're vegan (unless they already know). Also, inform your hosts that you're vegan from the start so that there's no awkwardness. Since food is a huge part of our culture, it's best to lay everything out to keep the air of positivity and enjoyment. Inform your hosts that you're not expecting them to go out of their way just to accommodate your lifestyle. Of course, if they do go out of their way, make sure to express your appreciation and gratitude to your hosts.

Part of being a good guest is being flexible too. If you aren't able to find a vegan-friendly establishment and it's obvious that everyone else is already getting hungry, tell them that you're okay with eating in any establishment. Then if the restaurant doesn't offer vegan fare, bring out your snacks and enjoy them along with your friends as they eat their meals. This will reduce any awkward situations and ensure that everyone is having fun. It also shows your companions that vegans aren't difficult to get along with just because you don't eat the same things they do.

7. Check which airlines offer vegan meals

If your travel involves flying from one place to another, check if the airline you're planning to fly with offers vegan meals. I've done some research myself and found out that these airlines offer vegan-friendly in-flight meals:

a. **American Airlines** offers vegan meals for flights with meal service. To request for this special meal, call at least 24 hours before your flight.

b. **Cathay Pacific** offers vegan meals as well which are high in iron, protein, and calcium.

c. **Qatar Airways** offers vegan meals as well which you may request upon booking or by giving them a call at least 24 hours before your flight.

d. **Singapore Air** offers vegan meals as one of the options when you book a flight with them.

e. **United Airlines** offers vegan meals as long as you put in your request at least 24 hours before your flight. You can do this by calling customer service or when you book the flight.

f. **Virgin Atlantic Airlines** also offers vegan meals upon booking or at least 48 hours before your departure.

8. Compromise with your companions

Just because you're vegan, that doesn't mean that everyone you travel with must follow you and eat the same foods you eat. Pushing this will make you a very unpopular travel buddy. You don't have to give up your own values, but there are several things you can do to travel with non-vegans.

Just like with relationships, learn how to compromise when you're traveling with your non-vegan friends and family members. Most non-vegans won't agree to dine at vegan restaurants. But you may compromise by agreeing to do something they want which you wouldn't normally do (unless it breaks your commitment to veganism) if they agree to dine at a vegan restaurant at least once. That way, you won't get left out with the activity you don't really want to do, and you'll get to eat at a vegan restaurant in return. It's another win-win situation!

9. Pack a lot of toiletries too

If part of your vegan lifestyle is only using vegan hygiene and beauty products, make sure to pack these too. Sometimes, such products are even harder to find than food items. Otherwise, you can also call the hotel before your trip to ask if they offer any vegan amenities. If they do, you won't have to pack the extra items.

10.   Use apps and other tools to your advantage

Another great way to prepare yourself is to use apps and other online tools. These days, restaurants make it a point to spread the word of their establishment through social media and food apps. Here are some recommendations which I've used in the past:

a. **HappyCow** allows you to search for recommendations for local vegan-friendly restaurants. The restaurant recommendations even come with photos and reviews from those who have already visited the establishments. If you really want to find the best vegan places to eat, HappyCow can be your best friend!

b. **Yelp** is another great app which is easy to use and which even has reviews for you to read about the vegan restaurants.

c. **VegGuide.org** allows you to perform a

search by airport, by continent or even by the type of restaurant you want to dine in.

d. **VeganTravel** allows you to browse vegan accommodations, activities, and restaurants all over the world. You can also see blogs and videos from the members of the vegan community.

e. **TripAdvisor** is very popular, and you can also use it to find vegan fare or restaurants which offer vegan-friendly foods.

Chapter 3
Surviving the Holidays with Your Non-Vegan Family

Who doesn't love the holidays? I certainly love every holiday as it's a chance for me to have fun with my loved ones. But back when I started my vegan journey, I had a lot of apprehensions during the holidays. Whether you're new to being vegan or you've been a vegan for some time now, the holidays always come with a challenge.

This is mainly because you will be interacting with family, friends, and loved ones who have a lot of questions about your lifestyle. Later on, we'll go through some of the most common questions non-vegans ask us vegans but, in this chapter, let's focus on surviving the holidays with the people you love so dearly.

Just because you're vegan, that doesn't mean that you should suffer through each and every holiday event you attend. The more you celebrate these occasions with your loved ones, the easier it will get. And the more open you are about your lifestyle, the more they will understand you.

The Happy-Compromise Strategy

When somebody asks you about your lifestyle, you may talk about it. Of course, don't start ranting about how non-vegans are wrong and all that. Doing this will just make the other person uncomfortable, and it may even confirm their beliefs that vegans are snobby, holier-than-thou people who have a very low opinion of others. We don't want that. Remember that you want them to understand you, support you, and accept you for who you are and the lifestyle you have chosen for yourself.

When you're planning to celebrate the holidays with your family, the best thing to do is have a happy compromise. Never push veganism on them and never demand them to make changes in their plans or in their menus just to accommodate your needs. The holidays are supposed to be happy events so trying your best to get along with everyone without compromising your own beliefs is always the best way to go. To help you survive, here are some practical and effective tips to keep in mind.

Bring a Vegan Dish Which Everyone Will Appreciate

Bringing a vegan dish to your holiday party is one of the best ways to help people understand that being vegan doesn't mean having to eat simple, plain or boring food.

Think about a dish that your family loves to eat during Thanksgiving, Christmas or any other holiday then volunteer to bring that dish. After that, try to find a vegan version of the dish for everyone to enjoy. It would be better for you to have a trial run of the dish to make sure that it tasted great and it will impress the guests.

Just because you'll celebrate the holidays with non-vegans, that doesn't mean that you don't get a say in terms of the menu. In fact, they will really appreciate you putting in the effort to create a vegan version of the traditional foods you eat during the holidays. And if you happen to whip up a killer dish, they might ask you for the recipe! Even if you don't (or can't) cook, you can search for vegan restaurants in your area where you can buy cooked dishes to bring to the party.

Clarify What You Can and Can't Eat

When you're talking about celebrating the holidays with your loved ones, remind them that you're vegan and make sure to do this in a friendly manner. If they don't know that you're vegan, you can introduce this during your conversation. Of course, they will have a lot of questions for you, one of which would be what you can't eat. Clarify the foods you can eat and the foods which you have eliminated from your diet. A lot of people don't really understand veganism, so it's helpful to be clear.

Of course, don't impose either. Tell the host or the cook about the food items you can't eat but ensure them that they don't have to change the whole menu just for you. If they ask you for some recommendations of vegan dishes, you may give some suggestions. You can also offer to help with the cooking, especially if the host is a member of your family or a close family friend. Letting them know beforehand is a lot better than announcing it at the table when there are no vegan-friendly options available. That would just be awkward!

Never Act as if Non-Vegan Food is Disgusting

Okay, this "tip" should be obvious. Still, it's worth mentioning. Even if you're vegan and you've sworn off specific foods, never EVER act as if the non-vegan dishes are disgusting. This will surely dampen the mood of your holiday. Think about it, how would you feel if you put in a lot of time, effort, and care to prepare a vegan dish for your family. But once you present it to them, they make disgusted faces or comments about the dish you were so excited to share with them. How do you think you would feel then? Personally, I'd probably walk out of the room, but that's just me!

No matter how much the non-vegan foods turn you off, telling the other guests or worse, the one who prepared the dishes that everything looks gross will just ruin the mood.

Also, saying these things will give them a bad impression of you and of vegans in general. So, don't ruin our reputation more! Besides, unless you were a vegan since you were born, you've probably eaten those same foods in the past too. So, if they gross you out now that you're vegan, try to think back when you used to enjoy those foods and maybe this will help you cope.

There's No Need to Have Vegan Talk at the Table

Another big no-no to avoid is to start vegan talk at the table. This is one mistake that I can talk about well because I myself did it. Imagine this, my family and I were having a great time one Thanksgiving. We were laughing, teasing each other, reminiscing, and generally having a good time. Then I made everything horribly awkward by saying something along the lines of, "Hey, don't you want to learn more about being vegan, so you can too stop eating dead animals? Really, it's a great lifestyle to follow!"

Then when I looked at the faces of my family members, I could tell that I just said the wrong thing. They started mumbling about how they support me and all that. They obviously didn't want to join the vegan bandwagon, but they didn't want to hurt my feelings either, even though I did hurt theirs. That's one mistake I'll never repeat again!

Sure, if someone asks you casually about veganism, you can answer casually too. But it's also not a good idea to go into the more harrowing reasons why you became a vegan in the first place such as animal torture or factory farming. No matter how calmly you explain these, everyone will definitely feel uncomfortable after you talk. So, it's better just to listen, talk about other things, and have fun with the conversations.

Host the Party Yourself

So you really want to enjoy the holidays with an elaborate vegan feast? The best way to do this is to host the party yourself. That way, you can prepare all the vegan dishes you want and let your non-vegan friends and family members be impressed by all of the scrumptious and healthy vegan dishes you prepare.

Of course, not everyone is up to the task of hosting their own party (but if you are, we'll talk about this more in Chapter 5). Remember that planning a party isn't a simple thing. But if you're comfortable with hosting, you love cooking, and you want your loved ones to have a truly vegan experience, then have at it!

Inform your guests that you'll only be serving vegan dishes so they should bring their appetites if they want. You can also allow your guests to bring their own dishes (whether homemade or store-bought) if they want to. At the end of the day, some guests may even want to bring home leftovers because the dishes are so delicious!

Talk About Vegan and Non-Vegan Foods to Educate Others

In one of the previous tips, I told you not to have any vegan talk at the table, especially elaborate and emotional discussions. But if someone asks you about it before the party or when things are winding down, don't be afraid to talk about your lifestyle choice either. The best thing to do is to talk about vegan and non-vegan foods for the purpose of educating others.

This topic is one of the safest topics to talk about, especially if someone just asked you about your being a vegan casually. Talk about the foods you eat, the foods you avoid, and how you've adjusted to veganism since you started. Then change the topic as casually as the other person brought it up.

Of course, you shouldn't assume that other people have a negative perception of veganism either. Some people ask questions because they're genuinely interested to learn about veganism. Don't miss this opportunity! When someone approaches you about veganism, try to determine whether they're only asking because they're curious or they really want to learn more about it because they're thinking about becoming a vegan too. On your end, always be positive, polite, and open to show that vegans are nothing like the common misconceptions.

Make a Game Out of It

Another great way to celebrate the holidays with your friends and family is to make a game out of it. As I said at the very start of this book (and I may mention this a couple of times more), don't take veganism too seriously. After trying to restrain yourself as much as you possibly can in the company of your non-vegan friends and family, it's time to talk to the other vegans you know.

When you have vegan friends, meet up with them once in a while for a good ranting or venting session. It's always better to have other people to talk to who share your beliefs and who also know where you're coming from. Us vegans should stick together, especially when it comes to encouraging each other to keep on going even though we don't find a lot of support from the ones we love or we're always experiencing challenges which make us want to quit.

Appreciate the Support and Effort No Matter How Little

So you've already talked to the ones you love about your lifestyle choice. Although they don't jump on the vegan bandwagon, if you see them making any kind of effort or give you any kind of support no matter how small, appreciate it and show them how thankful you are.

If they tell you that they don't eat bacon anymore, tell them how awesome that is! If they tell you that they've decided only to eat chicken and skip other types of meat, tell them how excited that makes you feel! If they made you a vegan-friendly version of their special salad, take a heaping serving of it (even though it's not that great). These small gestures are their way of showing you their support. So no matter how small the gesture is, appreciate it in a big way.

This is a lot better than telling people that they SHOULD follow the vegan lifestyle too. When you tell them that what they're doing or what they're eating isn't good, they probably won't listen to you. They might even feel that you're too pushy. So if you want them to support you, be encouraging and supportive too.

Try Placing Yourself in Their Shoes

When you attend holiday events with your family and friends, expect to get different reactions from them when they find out that you're a vegan. If they're encouraging, curious or supportive, good for you! But if they show aggressive behaviors towards this news, don't react the same way.

Try placing yourself in their shoes and consider why they're acting this way. Maybe they're feeling threatened by your lifestyle choice. Or maybe the realization that you've started and stuck with the vegan lifestyle is making them question their own lifestyle which, in turn, is making them defensive. For some people, they might even see your transition into veganism as a sort of insult to your family's cultures and traditions.

When you try to think about the reasons for their negative reactions, you will be able to react more positively. It's not a good idea to lose your temper and start preaching, especially during a holiday event. If you encounter such a reaction, just remind them gently that this choice you made was based on your own reasons. Ensure them that you're not rejecting or eliminating your family traditions, just the animal products.

Celebrate the Occasion!

Finally, celebrate the occasion! The reason for coming together as a family is to celebrate the holidays and enjoy each other's company. Christmas, New Year, Thanksgiving, and all the other holidays are a time to celebrate love, family, and food. This is not the time to convince your loved ones to become vegan too. It's also not the time to preach about veganism (in fact, there's never a good time to be "preachy" when it comes to veganism). Be polite, positive, happy, and don't let others bother you, even if they have some unkind things to say. As long as you're happy with your lifestyle choice, that's the important thing.

Chapter 4
When Attending Non-Vegan Birthdays or Dinners

Whether you're following a vegan diet, a vegetarian diet, a keto diet or any other diet out there, people will always be inviting you to birthdays, dinners, and other kinds of parties because they want to spend time with you. Of course, you'd definitely want to attend, and the worst possible thing that you can do is to turn down an invitation from family members, friends, and loved ones.

As a vegan, you want people to accept and support you by being open-minded. You can't do this by turning down every invitation you get just because you don't want to deal with the non-vegans in your life! Especially if you're the only vegan in your family or among your closest friends. You must understand that although you've chosen to go vegan, those around you may never make that same choice and that's okay. The important thing is that you have decided to change. But this doesn't have to mean that you should shut yourself out from the world because of it.

Don't Turn Down Invitations Just Because You're Vegan

One of the most challenging parts of becoming a vegan is how you will handle going to birthdays, dinners, and other parties as a vegan. For a lot of aspiring vegans, they're concerned about the many temptations present at parties (after all, the food is always AMAZING at parties) and they're afraid that they might go off track. For others (just like me at the beginning), they worry about what others might say or how others might perceive them at the party. It's always difficult to be the "weird" vegan at the party who isn't eating the food that's served.

But like I said earlier, you don't have to turn down every invitation you get just because you're vegan. Whether you're worried about yourself or the people around you, the best thing for you to do when you're invited to parties is to come up with a survival strategy. Here are some ways to do this:

Be Prepared

Whenever you attend parties, always prepare yourself to meet new people. Even if you're planning to go to a dinner party hosted by your mother and all your siblings are coming too, they might bring partners, friends, and other people whom you haven't met before. Therefore, the first thing you must do is be prepared. Remember that you're a vegan and some people don't really understand what veganism is and why people choose to become vegans. Also, remember that there's nothing wrong with this way of thinking.

Of course, when I say be prepared, I don't mean that you should prepare all the information and resources you can gather, so you're ready to argue with everyone at the dinner party. This just means that you should prepare for the reactions, questions, and curiosity of the guests at the party, especially those who don't know that you're a vegan. Don't feel defensive right away. Remember that some people just don't know much about veganism, but this doesn't mean that they're against this lifestyle.

If you're like me, you've probably done a lot of research about veganism before you decided to make the choice. Because of this, you've already prepared yourself adequately. Even more so if you've continued with your quest for learning even after you've begun your vegan lifestyle. Sometimes though, even after someone asks you about veganism and eating plant-based, this doesn't necessarily mean that they want to learn EVERYTHING that you know. No matter what type of question one of the guests asks you, this doesn't mean that you have to start talking about water pollution, cancer causes, animal abuse, and all the other effects of eating steaks.

Just answer the questions as casually as how the guest asked you. Fortunately for you, after you've read this book, you will be able to answer the most common questions asked by non-vegans more adequately and with a lot more confidence. Of course, I will be one of the first people to admit that preparing to deal with people at parties is very difficult, especially at the beginning. But at the right place and the right time (which means not at parties), you may talk about how incredible this lifestyle we've chosen is. Just, choose the time and place wisely.

Apart from dealing with the guests at parties, having to resist the temptation of food is a lot more difficult to deal with, especially when you've just started your vegan journey. Therefore, you must also be prepared to see, smell, and watch other people eat the foods you used to love but which you have consciously chosen to eliminate from your diet. One of the best ways to do this is to remember why you became a vegan in the first place as this can help motivate you to stick with your diet. Motivation is a very powerful tool. With the proper motivation, you will be able to stand up for yourself no matter how much you crave the foods served at the party or no matter how much they coax you into trying some "just this once."

Let Them Know

Okay, so I've advised you against going into a whole speech about veganism and being vegan when you attend parties. However, this doesn't mean that you shouldn't tell them that you're not vegan. In order to avoid any awkward situations, it's only proper to let them know that you're vegan. But by "them," I don't mean everyone, just the host. This is an important part of being prepared, especially when you're planning to attend parties with friends. From experience, if you attend parties with your family, they already KNOW that you're vegan. But say, a friend who you haven't connected with in a long time invites you over for dinner, it's only proper to let him/her know that you're vegan.

Think about it this way; if you have any kind of food allergies, you must say this to your host so that there's no risk of you eating anything which might cause you harm, you need to tell your host that you're allergic to the specific food items. This is a similar situation you must face when you're vegan. You need to let your host know of your diet (especially if you've just started) to avoid accidentally eating any dishes which contain non-vegan ingredients. You may even volunteer to bring a vegan dish or two in order to introduce your hosts or the other guests to vegan cuisine which you and I both know is delicious!

Introducing your host and the other guests to vegan cuisine is an excellent way to give everyone a good impression of veganism. Who knows? You might even plant the seed of interest in the vegan lifestyle. Let's face it, no matter what kind of diet you're on or what kind of foods you love to eat, we all have one thing in common, and this is that we all love delicious food! Letting them know that you're vegan and sharing your delicious food with them is an excellent way to change the common misconception in a silent but effective way. Rather than trying to convince everyone that vegan food isn't just "rabbit food," you should show them!

Honesty is always the best way to go. Being honest is a lot better than lying to your host or the other guests at the party about why you can't eat the food which is served. Imagine how awkward the affair becomes when they find out the truth? Then you have to explain WHY you lied, WHY you've chosen to go vegan, and all that jazz. But after finding out that you've lied, do you really think they will believe anything else you say?

Although this seems like an extreme situation, it does happen sometimes. I myself have experienced parties with awkward situations such as this and trust me; it's very hard to forget. So save yourself the embarrassment and just come clean. After all, being a vegan isn't anything to feel ashamed about! And the more you try to hide this fact, the more people will believe that it's not something to be proud of.

Don't Take it Personally

This is another important strategy that I will keep repeating over and over again. No matter how bad it gets, try not to take things personally! If other people ask you questions, answer them as if the issues don't have anything to do with your own ethics or beliefs even if you feel strongly about them. It's helpful to do this, especially when you're answering emotionally loaded questions, so you don't end up going into a whole tirade of how you made a choice to go vegan because you learned about the torture animals go through, how farming is destroying the environment, and so on.

The moment you take things personally, and you start taking what other people say about veganism against them, that's when things will start getting heated. Sure, this may be entertaining for some people, but when the communication starts to break down, and you're on the other end of it, you won't be feeling too celebratory after. In the end, you're the one who loses anyway. No matter how amazing your argument is, remember that you're in the company of non-vegans. So, if you keep on pushing them, you're the one who will look like a fool in the end. So, chill! Don't take things personally.

If you're a very emotional person, you may want to try separating yourself from the issue a bit at least for the time being. Before you leave your home, have a talk with yourself (don't do this in front of others!) and calm yourself down to prepare for all the questions you might encounter. You never know, the other guests might not even bring the subject up at all! But if they do, try answering their questions as casually as possible to make it seem like becoming a vegan was just one of the choices you've made in your life. If you don't make a big deal out of it, there's a lesser chance that other people will start calling you out because of it. But when you start getting preachy or pushy, they definitely won't appreciate that.

Even if some of the guests crack vegan jokes, just laugh along with them. As long as these aren't offensive, there's nothing wrong with laughing along once in a while. You may even want to learn a joke about meat eaters or two to retaliate in case the jokes start coming. Joking around doesn't make you any less of a vegan. But the good that comes out of this is that you won't make other people uncomfortable around you. And as you talk about your own journey into veganism, you don't have to comment about their food or lifestyle choices. Even though you've mastered the art of not taking things personally, some of the other guests might not. Since you don't want to offend anyone either, it's better to keep your thoughts about non-vegans to yourself. After all, there's no point in starting a battle when you're obviously outnumbered.

Have an Open Mind

This is the last strategy we will discuss in this chapter. Don't worry; there's more to come! After all, you need a whole arsenal of strategies in order to survive as a vegan in a world that's primarily non-vegan, right? The best kind of people are those who have an open mind. No matter who you are, what you do, what kind of lifestyle you're living, having an open mind will help you not only 'survive' but also to make more friends. It's never a good idea to judge the people around you, especially when you only base your judgment on the food they eat.

What's the point of creating your own opinion about another person's intelligence or what their purpose is in life just by looking at what they put on their plate? Personally, I have met plenty of non-vegans who care about the environment too. Conversely, I've also met a lot of vegans who've become vegan because they want to have better health. I have my own reasons for becoming vegan, and I'm sure you have yours too. So, you need to accept that other people who have started their journey into veganism have their own reasons which differ from ours. You might even meet non-vegans who, upon explaining why they will never become vegan, you might end up respecting even though they totally contradict your own beliefs.

Be careful though, having an open mind doesn't also mean that you will accept and believe what other people say. If you do this, you might end up doubting your own decisions! If you've decided to become a vegan, you also need to decide on why you adopt this lifestyle. This way you will you will feel strongly about why veganism is awesome.

Having an open mind means that you genuinely listen to other people and you accept who they are and what they believe in. This is a very important piece of advice, especially when you're attending parties with friends, family, and loved ones. Since you will be mingling with other people, you will be talking about different topics under the sun. And if you're good at changing the subject (a skill which comes in handy when somebody asks you a question about veganism and the conversation suddenly becomes awkward), the person you're talking to might start talking about his own lifestyle and beliefs. In such a case, you can practice your open-mindedness by not contradicting or arguing with the person you're talking to. Like I said before, just chill and have fun! It's a party after all!

Chapter 5
It's Your Birthday? Throw an Epic Vegan Birthday Party!

So, what do you do when your birthday is fast approaching? What else is there to do except throw an EPIC vegan birthday party? Birthdays are happy occasions where everyone's spirits are lifted with good company, great conversations, and incredible food choices. And just because you're vegan, that doesn't mean that you have to hold back when planning your own birthday party. In fact, this is the perfect time to show your guests just how tasty and versatile vegan dishes can be from your cake to your main courses, your desserts, and everything else in between.

Of course, birthdays aren't just about the food you serve. There's a lot to plan if you want to invite people over to your home to share this special day with. In this chapter, I'll be talking about the best-kept secrets which will transform your vegan birthday celebration to something so incredible that your guests will never forget it!

NOW It's All About You!

So, when you attended the parties hosted by other people, you had to be polite, deal with all the temptation coming from the food served and the people around you, and only eat a couple of the dishes which were vegan-friendly. But when it's your birthday, NOW it can be all about you. If it's your first birthday since you became vegan, you may feel both apprehensive and excited as you're planning. But before anything else, think of this as an opportunity to share your vegan lifestyle to the ones you love the most without having to force it down their throats.

Since it's your birthday, you'll be in charge of everything that will go on during the party. Of course, just because you're throwing a vegan party, ensure your guests that they won't have to "choke down" boring, bland food. This is the perfect time to introduce them to the more fun, interesting, and scrumptious side of veganism!

Set the Rules

If you're planning to have an all-out vegan party, make sure to set the rules for all your guests so that they know what to expect. If you don't plan to serve strictly vegan dishes, inform your guests of this. I won't lie to you; some of them will feel very relieved when they find out that you won't be serving only vegan dishes. But if you plan to only serve vegan fare, inform your guests of this fact too. As a vegan, you might not feel comfortable purchasing and cooking dairy or meat products with your kitchen utensils even if the dishes are for your family and friends. There's nothing wrong with this, of course, and (assuming that everyone you're inviting already knows that you're vegan), they don't expect this from you either.

Ensure your guests that even though you'll only be serving vegan fare, you're sure that each of the dishes will tantalize their taste buds. You can use whatever fancy wording you can think of to convince them that they will enjoy all the dairy-free and meatless dishes. As a side note, you can also allow them to bring their own snacks or dishes if they really want to make sure that they won't starve at your party (as if you would allow that to happen, right?).

Apart from the food, make sure that you've planned everything else in your party. If you have some games planned and the guests need to bring or think of anything for games, inform them beforehand. Just because you're throwing a vegan party, that doesn't mean that everything about the day will be vegan. I mean, it's not like part of the program would be a film showing about animal abuse, right? This is obviously a joke, of course. NEVER have a film showing about such horrid subjects during your birthday, or on any other party, you plan for your friends and family!

Simply put, you must start planning your party in advance. That way, you can come up with a good set of rules which you know won't offend anyone or make anyone turn down your invitation. Make sure that these rules are lighthearted, simple, and they aren't too pushy or laden with obligation. It's a party, after all. It's not a school activity where the guests have to follow strict rules, or they will be kicked out. As with any kind of party, make sure that your guests will still have a lot of fun even though they're feeling quite apprehensive about the food you're serving.

Drinks

Surprising as this may seem to a lot of people, there are some drinks which are non-vegan. When you're planning the beverage options, make sure you're serving both alcoholic and non-alcoholic drinks. For instance, if your birthday falls during the summer and you've planned a picnic or an outdoor party, serve some fresh drinks such as lemonade, juices, coffee, tea, mochitos, frozen daiquiris, and the like. If you plan to serve beers and wines, check the labels because not all of these alcoholic beverages are vegan.

While some people don't put a lot of thought into the drinks they serve during parties; this is one detail you can put a lot of thought into. Even though you're throwing a vegan party, you should offer a wide range of beverages to meet the needs of all your guests. For the alcoholic drinks, you don't have to go overboard, especially when it comes to cocktails. You may want to serve one or two signature cocktails and a couple of wine and beer options. For the other kinds of drinks, make sure that your guests will be able to drink a minimum of three glasses each of any of the beverages. This is a good way to estimate the number of drinks to acquire for your party.

One of the more popular vegan alcoholic drinks is white wine sangria. I myself am a huge fan of this drink, and I love serving it when I host parties. This drink has a lot of tasty ingredients including dry white wine (vegan, of course), raspberries, nectarines, orange juice (fresh), lime juice (fresh), and maple syrup. Just mix these ingredients together, chill in the refrigerator and serve to your guests! There are a lot of other vegan-friendly beverage concoctions available. Do a search online and you're sure to find a lot of different recipes.

Cake

Ah, cake. What is a birthday party without a cake? The great news is that there are so many vegan cake shops and cake recipes out there that this is one aspect which you won't have to feel stressed about when planning your birthday party. Go online, and you'll find endless recipes for vegan birthday cakes such as cheesecakes without cheese, chocolate cakes with avocado frosting, fluffy banana cakes, vegan carrot cakes, and so much more. I'm not kidding you; the list is endless! Even as you're reading this book, more and more vegans are coming up with new recipes and posting them online for other vegans to enjoy. It's quite amazing, really.

If you're good in the kitchen and you want your birthday cake to have a personal touch, it's best for you to bake the cake yourself. Not only will you be able to save a lot of money and choose only the best ingredients to use for your cake, but you will also impress all of your friends and loved ones as you serve the cake and tell them that it's your own creation. Of course, you may want to have a trial run first before you actually bake a cake for your birthday. That way, you're sure that the cake you will be serving on your special day will make them WANT to become vegans or at least explore more kinds of vegan-friendly cakes!

Even if you can't bake, you also have the option of purchasing a vegan cake from vegan bakeshops. This is a lot easier, especially if you plan to cook all of the other vegan dishes for your party. Either way, make sure that your birthday cake will be the center of attention as this is one of the most important and enjoyable parts of birthday celebrations.

Games and Activities

If you're planning your own birthday party, then you must make sure that it's going to be fun. Just because you're a vegan, this doesn't mean that everything about your party should focus on food. Although you'll be serving vegan food (which, let's face it, your guests might be scared of), you should make sure that they're all having fun. When this happens, it means that your party is a HUGE success. So part of your planning should involve thinking about games and activities to have at your birthday bash.

Games and activities are a great way to get your guests to relax and get into the party mood. Even if it's your birthday, if you see that your guests aren't having a good time, you won't be able to enjoy your party either. So make sure that the mood of your party is festive and light from the beginning. If you have a couple of guests who aren't vegan, your birthday party is neither the time nor place to convert them, judge them or even preach to them about veganism. For everyone to have a good time, you must make sure that all of your guests feel invited and comfortable.

Of course, if one of them asks about your lifestyle choice, you may start a conversation. But all you have to let your guests know is your own personal reasons for becoming vegan. You don't have to go into all of the other details. If your guests want more information, they might ask you more questions. Before the conversation gets too emotional or heated, casually offer your guest another slice of your delicious vegan cake!

Remember that birthdays should always be special, festive, and fun! After all, you only celebrate your birthday once a year. Here are some fun activities you may want to try with your guests at your party:

- **5-Second Animal**

    This is one game which you can play with your guests which is both fun and ironic since you're hosting a vegan birthday party. For this game, each of your guests has the chance to be a "judge." The rest of the guests get a piece of paper and a pen. For each round, the judge says the name of an animal then counts to five while the other players scramble to draw the animal in just a matter of 5 seconds. After counting, they all show their drawings to the judge, and he or she decides whose is the best one. It's a very subjective game that's also highly entertaining.

- **Balderdash**

  For this game, you need a collection of poems (if you want to stick with your vegan theme, try searching for poems around this subject), pieces of paper, and pens for all of your guests. Each player picks one of the poems and reads the first three lines of that poem out loud. Everyone writes down a fourth line for the poem and gives their lines to the player who read the poem. Then the reader reads all of the fourth lines. The winner of the round is the one who identifies the correct fourth line of the poem.

- **Telephone Pictionary**

  This is a hilarious twist on the traditional game which never, ever gets old. To prepare for this game, tear pieces of paper into small squares with the same size. Then create paper stacks wherein each of the stacks has an odd number of pieces of paper. The more pieces of paper you place into each of the stacks, the longer this game lasts and the funnier it will get!

  As the game starts, give each of the players a stack of paper. Then ask them to pick one piece and write down a sentence on their piece of paper. They can write anything down like "I like eating apples in my bathtub." The sillier, the better! After all of the players have written a sentence down, each the players will pass the paper stack to the player on their left. That player then reads the sentence, places the piece of paper at the very bottom of the paper stack, picks another piece of paper, and tries to draw a picture to illustrate the sentence.

After everyone has made their illustrations, they pass the piece of paper to the player on the left once more. Then they look at the illustrations, place the illustrations at the bottom of the paper stack, and write a sentence about the illustration that they saw. The game goes on and on until the pieces of paper on the stacks run out. Then you can all go through the stacks and see the funny illustrations and sentences together!

There are plenty of games and activities you can try with your guests at your party. You can modify some games, so they fit into a theme or just play the traditional games as is. Either way, games and activities are a lot of fun at parties.

Avoid Preachiness or Imposition of Your Vegan Lifestyle on Your Guests

Okay, so when your guests arrive, and the mood is starting to pick up, the last thing you want to do is preach or try to impose your vegan lifestyle on your guests. I mean, you're already serving them vegan food, and they're polite enough to eat it even though they're not really used to such dishes. This should be enough for you. Don't take it further by trying to shove your ideals and principles down their throats too! None of them will appreciate that, trust me. Just enjoy yourself!

When you're all at the table, introduce the different dishes you have prepared for them. As you're doing this, restrain yourself from food shaming, guilt-tripping or talking about the horrible abuse animals go through just to satisfy the taste buds of people who eat meat and meat products. Even if all of the foods on the table are delicious, your guests won't enjoy eating them if they're thinking about the crate rolling, force-feeding or other forms of animal abuse which you have described in your speech. You will never be able to convince non-vegans to become vegans if you make them feel guilty, uncomfortable or resentful towards you. In fact, they might even start having all of these negative feelings towards all other vegans, and that's not good.

You and I and all the other vegans in the world know that it's important to learn about the ordeal of the animals in food factories, companies, and farms. But never talk about this while people are eating! Even if not a single dish on the table contains animals or animal products. If your guests ask you about these issues, you can politely say that you don't want to get into all the details while you're at the table, but you can talk about it later if they really want to learn more about veganism. Answering this way will make your guests respect you since it shows that you understand that they also have boundaries.

It's bad enough that we already guilt-trip and shame ourselves for our food choices. But when the shaming and guilt-tripping come from other people, the effects are much more devastating. Never let other people feel bad about their lifestyles or the food choices they make. If you want to encourage others to go vegan, do it in a positive and enlightening way... and not during your party!

Chapter 6
Meal Prep

These days, preparing homemade meals can be very challenging, especially if you have a day job, you have a family to take care of, or you have other tasks which keep you busy all day, every day. This is one common reason why a lot of people aren't able to stick to a healthy diet. If you're not able to prepare your meals for the day because you don't have time and there aren't a lot of vegan restaurants in your area, you can either skip your meals until you get home (which isn't healthy), or you can give in and dine out with your friends even if this means eating in restaurants which don't offer vegan-friendly fares.

The good news is that there is a thing called meal prep or meal prepping. This means that you would set aside a whole day of the week (I do this every Sunday) where you would prepare all of your meals and snacks for the week. Meal prepping is not a new concept. A lot of people do this, especially those who follow special diets. I myself started meal prepping a couple of months after I started becoming a vegan. I started preparing my meals not because I had no choice. In fact, I'm lucky enough to live in an area where there are a lot of vegan-friendly restaurants and shops. Eventually, though, I came to realize that meal prepping is a lot more economical and a lot more fun (at least for me).

So, no matter how busy you are, meal prepping can help

you out a lot, especially in terms of sticking with your vegan diet. In this chapter, we'll be talking about meal prepping more because this is one of the best and most effective survival strategies, I can think of sharing with you.

Why It's Important

Without meal prepping (and the other helpful tips in this book), you might find it quite challenging to follow a healthy and balanced vegan diet. Just like when you're on the road, you should do research, and plan for everything you will eat from the start to the end of your trip. This is basically the same in your daily life. Meal prepping will make your life easier in the long run, especially once you get the hang of it.

Even if you're lucky enough to live in an area with a lot of vegan-friendly restaurants, farmer's markets, and groceries which offer vegan food items, buying your food from these establishments each and every day, you'll be spending too much in the long-run. But if you purchase fresh ingredients and use these to whip up healthy, delicious, and vegan-friendly dishes, you'll be able to save a lot of money. Fresh ingredients are a lot cheaper than cooked dishes and processed "vegan" food items. And if you already own basic kitchen utensils and appliances, you're all set!

As I've mentioned earlier, meal prepping involves you spending a couple of hours whipping up meals and dishes for a certain number of days. If you work from Monday to Friday, you can do your meal prepping on the weekends. But if you have a more irregular schedule, you can set one or two days each week to prepare your food for the rest of the days. Either way, you will have to set aside some time for the purpose of planning, preparing, and cooking your meals which you will store in your refrigerator to keep them fresh.

Apart from being able to save a lot of money on food, meal prepping allows you to focus on other things. When I started my vegan journey, I spent A LOT of time thinking about and worrying about where my next meal will come from, especially when I was at work. Sure, there were a lot of restaurants around the area, but there were a lot of times when I was craving for home cooked meals. There were also times when I skipped meals at the beginning of the day because I was already running late, and I didn't have time to prepare my breakfast. I also missed a lot of dinners because I was too tired to prepare or cook anything when I got home.

So yeah, it was definitely a challenge for me. So a couple of months after starting my vegan journey, I learned about meal prepping and things got better from there. Meal prepping can help you follow the vegan lifestyle better no matter how tired or busy you are. In fact, you'll even start looking forward to your meals, especially if you've prepared some of your favorite dishes on your meal prep day. So if you haven't started meal prepping yet, try it out for yourself. It does take some getting used to but the more you do it, the better you become at it and the easier and more fun meal prepping will become for you.

How to Plan Your Meals

When it comes to meal planning, there are several ways you can go about it. Go online, and you'll get all of the inspiration you need to learn how to plan your meals. If this is your first time to even learn about meal planning, there's a lot for you to learn. Don't worry though, meal planning is an interesting and enjoyable venture. After some time, you'll see yourself becoming a huge meal prepping fan. So here are some tips to start you off:

- First of all, decide whether you want to do your meal prepping once or twice a week. Like I've said before, if you work during the weekends, you may want to do your meal prepping on one of your days off. But if you have an irregular schedule where you may also work on weekends, you may do your meal prepping twice a week.

- Once you've decided your meal prepping schedule, you should prepare further by purchasing all of the items you need for your meal preps. If you already have cooking utensils and appliances, all you have to buy are the containers to store your prepped meals in. If not, then you may have to buy a LOT of stuff.

- When it's time for meal prep, make sure you're having fun doing it. As you wash, chop, and cook in your kitchen, make things more fun by playing some music, a podcast, audiobook (like this one) or putting on your favorite television show. Do this as part of your routine, and you'll definitely love your meal prepping time.

It's that easy! But if you're a beginner, you might feel overwhelmed with everything you need to do and everything you need to think about. So here are more tips for you, this time more practical tips for when you're meal prepping:

- Before preparing your meals, plan everything first. You can do this whenever you have free time before you do your shopping. And when it's time to shop for your ingredients, bring your list along and make sure you stick to it!

- If you're new to meal prepping, start with the meals you know how to make. If you're totally new to meal prepping or cooking, for that matter, then you should do your research first before you start! There are plenty of online resources which can provide you with all of the recipes and meal prep ideas you need. My all-time favorite place for recipe-inspiration is

Pinterest. Boy, this place is a vegan-chef hub! If you want to check on some really good ones, go to Pinterest and look up _The Savory Vegan_ and _The Curious Chickpea_.

- Frozen produce is your friend. Frozen veggies and fruits are an excellent part of meal prepping. These are very affordable, they come fresh, they pack a ton of nutrients, and they fit right into your vegan diet. Also, most of these already come pre-chopped so you don't have to do a lot of prepping when using these. I always have plenty of frozen berries, bananas and spinach which are the main ingredients of my breakfast smoothie. I also stock up on edamame beans, green beans and peas which I like to add to my salads – they add an extra protein-kick.

- Apart from preparing entire meals and dishes, why not try making your own condiments too? If you love eating salads (which is a great thing regardless of your diet), you can make the sauces and dressings ahead of time then keep them in your refrigerator. These condiments can last for up to 7 days when stored in the refrigerator. So when you have some free time, all you need to do is chop up some raw veggies, prepare other healthy ingredients, and add your condiments!

- Each week, try to plan for meals which have similar ingredients. That way, you won't have to purchase a lot of different ingredients when you go shopping. This is also a great hack if you aim to minimize your food waste. Sometimes when we shop, we do that with the eyes, and we buy more products than we need, and often they end up in the waste container. Personally, I feel such a guilt when wasting food, not only because it affects my budget, but also because this was something my parents were very strict about. My brother and I were taught to respect the food and to not buy more than we can eat.

- After meal prepping, you would store your meals in your refrigerator or freezer to keep them fresh up until it's time for you to eat them. Foods which are stored in your refrigerator will last for up to 3 days. So if you're prepping meals for the whole week, you should place the meals which you will be eating during the end of the week in the freezer so they'll last longer.

- After meal prepping, make sure to completely cool down the meals you've made before you place the lids and store them in the refrigerator or the freezer. When you place warm foods in the fridge, this increases the temperature which, in turn, places the other food items at risk of getting spoiled.

- Before you eat one of the meals you have prepared, check it using of your senses first. Check how it looks and how it smells too. It's not a good idea to taste the foods if you're trying to check if your meals are still good.

- Reheat your food properly. If you want to eat your meal hot, then reheat it thoroughly. Make sure that your meal is heated all the way to the middle to avoid the risk of bacteria thriving on it.

- Even if you've decided to prep your meals each week, you may leave a night or two each week off. Although this isn't a requirement, it's highly recommended. That way, you can enjoy a couple of fresh meals every week.

How Not to Waste

Just because you've gone vegan, that doesn't mean that you won't be wasting any food. As I said, I've done this quite a few times and we're probably all guilty of this. Whether we eat at home or dine out, we sometimes end up wasting a lot of food. When I started meal prepping, I seldom brought a shopping list with me. Because of this, I ended up buying too many ingredients, and I wasn't able to use a lot of them before they spoiled.

Actually, food waste is very common for vegans because we usually purchase fresh ingredients such as fruits and vegetables (which is why you should consider the frozen varieties). Then when your friends call you over for lunch or dinner, the fresh produce you've bought ends up wilting in your refrigerator. This is a very common scenario. So just like your choice to become vegan, if you've decided on meal prepping, stick with your routine. This is also one reason why it's a good idea to leave a meal or two out of your meal preps. So, if anyone invites you to eat out, you don't have to turn them down. Here are more tips to help you minimize or even eliminate food waste:

- I've said it before, and I'll say it again. Make a list before you shop for ingredients and other food items. This will help you focus on what you need to buy each time to go shopping. The list also allows you to only buy what you need for the meals you've planned.

- Before shopping, check your stocks first. If you have any leftover ingredients from last week, use them for the dishes you'll prepare for the coming week. After shopping, use up all of the fresh herbs and produce first.

- If, after your prep, you end up with bits and pieces, don't throw these out. Store them and get creative for the next week. Think about or research some dishes where you can use the bits and pieces which you weren't able to use. You can whip up a delicious soup almost from everything. When I have a bit potatoes, broccoli and mushrooms left, I throw them in a pot with boiling vegie bullion, and top with fresh parsley.

Meal Prep on a Budget

Ah, the budget. One of the reasons why a lot of people believe that veganism isn't worth trying. Because they believe that living a vegan lifestyle is too expensive. In reality, though, it's not. Even more so when you meal prep. Instead of dining out which can be very expensive, especially if you order vegan-friendly dishes, purchasing fresh ingredients and whipping up scrumptious meals is actually more economical. If you really want to meal prep on a budget, here are some tried-and-tested tips which I also use when meal prepping:

- Think about some meal prep staples which you will frequently have such as beans, rice, lentils, chickpeas, and quinoa. These are very affordable, and you can use them in different ways or in creating different dishes.

- When it comes to meal prepping while on a budget, the seasonings will play a huge role. Adding seasonings, herbs, and spices to your dishes will make them more flavorful without having to add expensive ingredients. I have found out that mint goes well with beans and bulgur, dill is great when added to green beans and thyme complements very well dishes with green lentils.

- Rather than getting fresh produce, go for the frozen kind. These are more affordable, and they contain just as many nutrients as fresh produce. Plus, if you're not able to use these frozen ingredients, they won't spoil right away.

- Go for dried beans instead of canned ones. These are healthier and a lot cheaper too. Just make sure to soak the dried beans the night before your meal prep day so that they're ready for cooking. I try to always soak beans for the full 24 hours instead of just overnight. After soaking, be sure to thoroughly drain and rinse the beans until all the scum is washed away. Fill the pot with fresh filtered water, bring to a boil, and skim away any additional foam that may come to the top at the start of the boil. A trick I learned from my granny is to change the water once again once it begins to boil. Once you bring the new water to boil, turn down the heat to a simmer, season, and cook until the beans are soft (about 4 hours). Drain beans and add to your favorite dish or let cool and freeze in large freezer bags for quick meals at a later date.

- In terms of your meal prep containers, I find that glass containers are a lot better in the long-run. They're sturdy, you can reheat your food in the microwave, and they won't smell like your previous dishes over time. These are more economical and better for the environment too compared to their plastic counterparts.

- Mason jars are great too, especially if you love salads, soups or any other kind of layered food you want to prepare. Investing in a couple of glass mason jars is a good idea. Plus, smoothies look way more exclusive in mason jars, rather than in regular glasses.

Another way you can save while meal prepping is to think of dishes which are tasty, versatile, and which require cheaper vegan ingredients. Here are some examples of affordable but tasty meals that I absolutely love prepping;

- Overnight oats are cheap, easy to prepare, and there are SO MANY ways to make them. Depending on your budget, you can add different ingredients to the oats to make a healthier and more filling meal. Try adding nuts, crushed flax seeds, fresh fruits, plant-based milk and cinnamon.

- Breakfast bowls are great too. Choose the right combination of ingredients, and your breakfast bowl can be both hearty and flavorful enough that you won't go hungry for a couple of hours.

- Speaking of bowls, vegan burrito bowls are AMAZING too. There are plenty of recipes online, each of them more mouthwatering than the previous. If you're a fan of Mexican food, this dish is definitely one to consider.

- Have you ever tried pasta packs? This is when you prepare and freeze pre-cooked packs of whole-wheat pasta then pair these with single servings of pasta sauces for breakfast, lunch or dinner. They're easy to prepare, they're healthy, and there are so many options for you to choose from!

- Speaking of packets, why not try smoothie packets too. Preparing them is the same as preparing pasta packs. All you have to do is prepare individual servings of smoothie ingredients and store them in the refrigerator. Then all you have to do is throw all of the contents of the packets in the blender, and you're good to go.

As you can see, meal prepping is both easy and economical. The more you do this, the easier it becomes and the more creative you will become in terms of planning your meals and preparing different dishes. Soon, you might even discover that you have a real talent for cooking!

Chapter 7
Limiting Beliefs

One of the saddest things about being a vegan is that a lot of people have a negative perception of plant-based eating. But what's even sadder is that sometimes, we ourselves earn that reputation. People either see us as pretentious hippies who are just "following the trend," or they chastise us for being "overly self-righteous" and preachy when it comes to our lifestyle and dietary choices. While a lot of us just want our family and friends to support us, sadly, a lot of vegans are obnoxious about it. So who can blame others for having a bad perception of us, right?

The Most Frustrating Beliefs About the Vegan Lifestyle

Of course, just because you know that other people don't appreciate vegans, that doesn't mean that you should just accept this fact and allow them to have a negative perception of you and of the lifestyle you've chosen. For most people, they believe anything they hear without even confirming the source. Because of this, there are a lot of beliefs about vegans and veganism, some of which are just downright frustrating!

So if you're talking to someone about being a vegan and they say these things to you, don't snap back at them right away. In most cases, they're just trying to convince themselves that veganism isn't something to consider. They're not TRYING to be offensive. It's just that they've heard these beliefs from someone else in the past and so they've made those beliefs their own as well. If you've been confronted with this situation, here are some explanations you can give the non-vegans in your life.

#1 - "I'll have to eat boring food like salads without flavor for the rest of my life!"

This is one of the most common beliefs people have about vegans. That we only eat "boring" salads all our lives. This is also why a lot of people believe that we eat nothing but "rabbit food." Of course, this is far from the truth. Sure, we do eat a lot of salads, but they're never boring. I have always loved eating salads, and since I started learning how to make different kinds of salads, I love them even more! There are so many types of ingredients you can add to your vegan salads to make them more interesting, healthier, and more delicious!

And our vegan options don't stop there. We also eat burgers, chocolate, burritos, tacos, pasta, smoothies, pizza, falafels, and so much more. As a matter of fact, eating vegan or plant-based foods is never boring. That is unless you've never done research before about the other kinds of dishes you can eat while you're a vegan. If this is the case, then it's time for you to go online and enrich your life with the endless choices out there.

So if someone says something like this to you, share all of your wonderful experiences with food. Throughout your vegan journey, you'll come to learn about different types of vegan foods and dishes which you didn't even know existed! For instance, did you know that you can use tofu to make ricotta cheese? You can even make macarons using the water from boiled or canned chickpeas! If you're a fan of chocolate mousse, why not try making it with roasted sweet potatoes or ripe avocados? These are just three examples for you, imagine how much more you can learn from cookbooks and online resources! So, if someone tells you that he or she doesn't want to go vegan because he or she doesn't want to eat boring salads for the rest of his life, restrain yourself from rolling your eyes. Instead, share your own experiences and the favorite foods you eat.

#2 - "I can't give up cheese."

Ah, cheese. That ooey, gooey, creamy food item which I used to love. Just like most people, I couldn't get enough of cheese. In fact, I always used to order extra cheese whenever I ordered burgers. The fact is, cheese is one of the most addicting foods out there. And once you accept that you're addicted to it as I had done, you will be able to break free of your addiction. Soon, you'll realize that you don't even crave it anymore even if you see other people eating it.

Cheese is so darn addictive because of its extremely high concentration of casein, a type of milk protein. When your body digests this milk protein, this results in the production of casomorphins (I know, it's such a scientific term!). Surprising as this may seem, casomorphins are a type of opioid which belongs to the same chemical family as opium and morphine. And when the casomorphins spread throughout your body, they start lowering pain and inducing feelings of euphoria. When I found out about this, I thought to myself, "no wonder I couldn't get enough of the stuff!"

But just like opium and morphine casomorphins are highly addictive. So if you suddenly quit eating cheese, you might experience strong cravings and even some uncomfortable withdrawal symptoms. Unlike the other types of dairy products, cheese loses a lot of water when it's processed which makes it very high in protein. So the more cheese you eat, the mote casomorphins are produced and thus, the harder it will be for you just to give up this particular addiction.

So, when someone tells you that he or she just can't give up cheese, you can casually give him or her this explanation. Then share your own experiences of how you "broke the addiction" and how you now enjoy a healthier, kinder, and more delicious diet which you absolutely love, and which doesn't contain cheese. Of course, you wouldn't be able to convince cheese lovers right away so keep an open mind about this. And don't talk about abused cows because this is a big turn-off. Instead keep the focus on the health benefits of ditching *parmigiano*.

#3 - "I am actively doing sports, and I need animal protein."

Since vegans follow a plant-based diet, a lot of people believe that it will make them weaker. Because of this, those who actively do sports or those who enjoy working out regularly don't want to go vegan because they believe that they need animal protein. But if this was true, how can you explain the success of Patrik Baboumian, the strongest man in Germany; James Southwood, the French Kickboxing World Champion; or Serena and Venus Williams, the best tennis players of all time? One thing they have in common is that they are all vegans.

There are a lot of athletes who are powered by a plant-based diet who are strong, always have a high performance, and are at the peak of health. The key is to plan your plant-based or vegan diet well to ensure that you're getting all of the nutrients your body needs to be able to keep up with the sports or any other physical activities you regularly do.

It's actually funny to see how people react when they realize how strong vegans can be. From doing sports, exercising at the gym regularly, and doing daily chores, there's a lot that we can do! When someone talks to you about this particular point, they really feel shocked when you talk about how strong you are even though you only eat plant-based foods. To be honest though, for me, I haven't seen any changes in terms of my gym performance and my strength since I started on my vegan journey. But for some people, they've definitely experienced a change for the better, especially those who know how to choose the healthiest food options to keep their strength up. Of course, if you only eat "vegan-friendly" junk foods, you're definitely going to see yourself getting weaker by the day. As I've said, the key is to plan your diet well and always remember to eat smart.

#4 - "I'll have to take a bunch of supplements and vitamins."

Okay, this point is a bit more challenging to talk about with non-vegans, especially since a lot of vegans do take plenty of supplements and vitamins. But here's the down-low: a proper vegan diet provides you with all of the necessary ingredients you need for optimal health. That is when you eat a wide range of healthy plant-based foods such as seeds, greens, legumes, fruits, vegetables, and some types of fortified foods. This makes it more complete and a lot closer to non-vegan diets. The only difference is that you don't eat any animal-based foods as part of your daily diet.

A concern of non-vegans is that if they go vegan, they won't be able to get all of the nutrients they need to stay healthy and avoid any deficiencies. But this can also happen to people who follow other diets without eating the proper foods to get all the nutrients they need.

Both non-vegans and vegans may take supplements and vitamins to prevent deficiencies and make sure that they're getting all of the nutrients they need to function optimally. Whether you're a vegan or a non-vegan, you should include fortified foods in your diet to ensure healthy living. The manufacturers of these types of foods incorporate supplements to their products so that you can get all the nutrients, vitamins, and minerals you need. Basically, it's all about how you plan your meals.

For instance, there are vegan-friendly milk products which are fortified with vitamins A, D3 and K2. Or some vegan cheese and tofu products which are fortified with vitamin B12. There are a lot of options for you to choose from. Deciding on what kind of supplements you want to implement in your diet involves a lot of research. This can be quite fun because you will learn more about the lifestyle you've chosen and why your body needs what it needs. I personally have always been taking supplements, even before going vegan. The only vitamin I added to my usual supplement stack after adopting a plant-based diet is B12.

#5 - "People will think of me as a weirdo and even my family wouldn't support me."

This is another statement which makes a lot of vegans roll their eyes when they hear it. I mean, even after I typed the statement, I rolled my eyes and chuckled. Sadly though, this is one thing non-vegans really worry about when they're considering the vegan lifestyle. If someone approaches you with this concern, the best thing you can do is reassure them that this isn't something he or she should be worrying about.

The more you speak to the ones you love about being a vegan, the more their image of a barefooted, chakra-opening, granola-eating hippie vegan will start fading away. The more you share your views, stories, and experiences with the people around you, the more they will learn to accept you and the lifestyle you've chosen. Of course, you shouldn't expect the change or the acceptance to happen overnight. Although some people may think of you as a "weirdo," in time, your friends, family, loved ones, and the people who matter to you will accept this change, respect you for making a choice and sticking to it, and even show their genuine support to you. When this happens, you will feel more empowered and prouder of yourself for standing your ground despite all the challenges.

Expect that some of the people around you will still ask you a lot of questions mainly because they're curious about veganism and they want to learn more. In such cases, reply politely and never try to make them feel bad about their own lifestyle or dietary choices. As Mahatma Gandhi once said, "Be the change you want to see in the world." So simply start with yourself, and you will gradually change the minds and perspectives of the people around you.

#6 - "Friends will stop inviting me or refuse to come over for dinner."

Sadly, this is a possibility, especially for people who don't want to open their minds and accept people who are different from them. But when you think about it, do you need such people in your life? One of the things I've learned by becoming a vegan is that a lot of people have a hard time changing their views of vegans as judgmental, preachy, self-righteous people who are just plain picky about the foods they eat.

When you encounter people like this, you can either feel discouraged, upset, or angry at them. Neither of these reactions will help you on your journey. Think about it: if you're already having a hard time with the change you've decided to make and you're stressing yourself out more by pressuring your friends and family to accept you, how do you think the situation will play out? Most likely, you'll just give up altogether and go back to your old non-vegan ways.

Don't be "that guy." Seriously. If you've convinced yourself that the vegan lifestyle is what's best for you, stick with it! We've all been there. We've all experienced the hardships. If you don't want to avoid alienating yourself from those around you, here are some tips to help you out:

- Never, ever preach about veganism, especially when you're invited to dinner by a non-vegan. Instead, inform the one who invited you about your diet and offers to bring a vegan dish so he or she won't feel stressed about what to serve you. If the host insists on cooking a vegan dish for you, make sure to express your gratitude and appreciation for the effort.

- While having dinner, don't tell the guests how they should eat. No matter how excited you are about this new change in your life, if they aren't asking about it, they probably don't want to hear about it. When I became vegan, I remember the urge to tell people 'the truth'. It felt like I discovered something that everybody has the right to know and I should not keep it to myself. Unfortunately, this is not how people will interpret your passionate speech about animal welfare and cancer prevention. Try to not volunteer information at occasions not meant for discussing eating habits and ethics. Starting conversation like this is as bad as talking about religion or politics at the table.

- While some friends or family members might ask

you about your lifestyle choice, don't feel offended if they don't even bring up the topic. Maybe they're not yet ready to talk about veganism with you.

As long as you don't push your beliefs and principles on your friends and family members, they'll see that it's okay to keep inviting you over. You don't have to change who you are and how you interact with others when you become a vegan. The biggest change you're making is the foods you choose to eat. So, don't let this affect your social life.

#7 - "Being vegan is hard; I will be starving all the time."

Honestly, the only time I remember going hungry as a vegan was that time when I went on a trip with my friends, and I didn't prepare for it. After that, I've always managed to stay on top of my food game. Since plant-based foods generally contain more fiber than dairy or animal-based foods, this means that they're a lot more filling. Since we eat a lot of nuts, beans, fruits, and vegetables which are chocked full of fiber, I don't understand why people think that being a vegan means starving all the time. In fact, I usually feel pleasantly satisfied and full after my meals. Plus, I don't get to experience the feeling of being sleepy after eating. This can be a natural result of digestion meat and dairy.

Of course, I'm not saying that shifting from an animal-based to a plant-based diet is an easy thing. But once you try it, you may see that it's easier than what you expected. As long as you know the reasons why you became a vegan in the first place, there's a higher likelihood that you'll succeed. Soon, you'll come to realize that you are at peace with the lifestyle you've chosen. Even if you go into a restaurant or other food establishments which don't have vegan-friendly options, you won't feel upset. As long as you know that the vegan lifestyle is the best choice for you (and for the planet too!), you won't see it as a "hard" thing.

Chapter 8
Debunking Veganism Myths

"A lie gets halfway around the world before the truth has a chance to get its pants on." - Winston S. Churchill

Although I've already come to accept how "closed-minded" some people are about veganism, it's still very frustrating to keep explaining the same thing over and over again to different people each time you tell them that you're a vegan. The reason for the common perception of people about us vegans is the different myths which have been started by some careless persons, but which have endured. Each time a person hears these myths and shares them to others, they become stronger and more widespread. So how do we deal with this? Well, the best thing we can do is to extend our patience and try to explain the truth to those who want to listen. Don't worry though; it gets easier each time you get to debunk one vegan myth after another. Hopefully, the more we do this, the more people will start questioning these myths too.

The Most Ridiculous Veganism Myths

A lot of times, you will have to deal with people saying the most ridiculous things about your lifestyle. Don't take it personally though, I've also heard them saying ridiculous (sometimes even offensive) things about the diets and lifestyles of other people. Let's face it; there are just some people out there who only believe in their own principles. So if they hear other people speak of new ideas, concepts, and beliefs, they tend to shun all of these because they don't share the same perspectives.

This is a normal thing you would have to deal with. If you never experienced speaking to such people, good for you! But if you encounter these people or these situations, the best you can do is provide enlightenment in a lighthearted and positive way. To help you out, let's debunk some of the most common myths about vegans and veganism together.

Myth #1 – Vegans are Hippy Enlightened Yogis

First, there is nothing wrong in being enlightened yogi and I never get offended if people think this of me. And although a lot of vegans do enjoy meditation and yoga, this doesn't mean that ALL vegans are yogis or are into spirituality. Just like non-vegans, vegetarians, followers of the keto or paleo diet, and more, vegans are made up of all kinds of people of different ages, both genders, and varying education, nationality, sexuality, profession, and religion. Vegans like you and me come in all shapes and sizes, and we all come from different walks of life.

So, when someone asks you if you're a hippy or a yogi, you don't have to be offended. But you don't have to just nod and accept those titles either. You can help debunk this particular myth by explaining to the person who asked you why this myth doesn't really apply to all vegans on the planet. As I've been saying over and over again, some people have their own prejudices or assumptions about vegans and veganism. But when you get down to the basics, vegans are just people who don't eat animals or animal products. We also don't wear anything which required the exploitation or abuse of animals. It's as simple as that.

But for some people, being a vegan means wearing clothes made of hemp, skipping shaving or spending the whole day upside down on a yoga mat. Also, a lot of people believe that vegans are always malnourished and skinny (more on this point later on). When someone shares these beliefs with you, ask him or her if you're all that he or she described. Obviously (unless you happen to be a skinny yogi who falls within all of these descriptions in which case, good for you), when the person looks at you, he or she will immediately realize that the image they have of vegans might not be too accurate.

After the realization, you can talk about the diversity of

vegan people. Being a vegan isn't like being part of a specific race or ethnicity. Anyone can be a vegan as long as they accept the lifestyle and the diet we are supposed to follow. If you know any other vegans (celebrities or other people you both know), you can talk about them too. This way, you're giving a concrete example of "real people" who are far from the stereotype. Simple as this explanation is, it will help clarify the situation which, in turn, debunks the myth that all vegans are enlightened, hippy yogis.

Myth #2 – We are Supposed to Eat Meat

Historically speaking, there were many times, when people had no choice but to hunt their meal and eat meat in order to survive. Even now, there are populations in some countries who must depend on livestock, poultry or fish to get the calories and protein they need to thrive. Some of the coastal areas don't have enough land to support farming, but they have easy access to huge amounts of fish and other seafood. While a lot of people had to depend on meat for their survival both in the past and in some parts of the world now, this isn't really the case for the majority.

Now, there are so many foods and food items available in supermarkets, farmers markets, restaurants, and other food establishments that we don't have to go out and hunt for our next meal. With regards to nutrition, there's nothing you can find in animal-based foods and animal products which you can't also find in a vegan diet that's well-planned and researched. If you didn't grow up as a vegan, it's natural for you to crave certain foods which you have been eating all your life. For most of us, animal products have always been a part of our traditions and our past history. But this doesn't mean that we are SUPPOSED to eat meat.

Just like the tradition or the need to eat meat, there are a lot of things which used to be part of our past that we don't do now. Some examples include not allowing women to vote or to have an education, rich people owning slaves, human zoos (imagine if these were still a thing!), discrimination (sadly this is still a thing for some people), and so much more. We successfully got rid of these horrid things which used to be the norm of our ancestors. Some of them even lasted for centuries! That is until we started to know better and realize that all these things weren't right.

So maybe it's time for us to realize that just because we're so used to eating meat, this doesn't mean that we're supposed to do it. We're not lions, tigers or other kinds of predators who have a natural instinct to kill other animals and devour their flesh. We're supposed to be the "intelligent" species, right? This means that we always have a choice. We can decide whether we would like to continue eating meat or follow a healthier, plant-based diet that doesn't cause harm to animals (and to the planet for that matter).

Myth #3 – Cows Need to be Milked, and We are Actually Doing Them a Favor

I still remember the time when someone told me this particular point. Personally, I never heard of this, so it really surprised me. Weird as this myth is, a lot of people have heard it and believed it. I don't really know who started this myth, but if you're from the city and you don't know anything about farm animals, you might actually believe that cows need to be milked and doing this is actually beneficial for them.

But the truth is, farmers need to milk their cows because they take the calves away from their mothers. Then they feed the calves with a replacement formula which isn't as healthy as their mother's milk because it's made from vitamins and slaughterhouse plasma. After some months, the milk of the cow yields peak. When this happens, they re-impregnate the cows to restart the entire cycle. Now try to imagine this being done to human beings. When you think about it, this is a very sad and terrible life these cows have. They're used to provide milk to humans while their babies are taken away from them while they're still young.

The worst part is that it doesn't end there. These cows are also forced to live in crowded sheds where they often pick up diseases. One of the most common diseases suffered by these cows is mastitis. This is a type of infection of a cow's udders which is caused by too much milk yields of dairy cows. Seriously, don't believe anyone who tells you that a cow's udder will explode if farmers don't milk them, because a cow would never find herself in this situation if her calve isn't taken away.

The good news is that it's actually quite easy to give up milk and other dairy products. Nowadays, there are some incredible vegan versions of these dairy products, and you can find them in local grocery stores and farmer's markets. These shops offer different kinds of vegan milk such as those made from hazelnut, almond, coconut, rice, and soy. There are also a lot of vegan ice cream and cheese options out there if you know where to look.

Myth #4 Humans Need Animal Protein Because Plant-Based Protein Isn't Complete Protein

Have you ever heard of "complete proteins?" This is derived from the fact that there are 20 kinds of amino acids which form proteins. Unfortunately, our bodies cannot produce 9 of these amino acids on their own. Therefore, a complete protein is one which contains all of these 9 essential amino acids and in equal amounts. But we don't really need to consume this entire amino acid profile each time we eat a meal. Our bodies only require an adequate amount of each of these amino acids each day.

This myth started because of the idea that you can only get protein from meat. Of course, we know that this isn't so.

Although animal sources contain proteins, they often contain cholesterol and saturated fats too which aren't good for the body. On the other hand, plant-based food sources which contain protein such as quinoa, nuts, beans, tofu, and others, are a lot healthier. Plant protein isn't incomplete neither is it inadequate. In fact, it's even better because it's cholesterol-free, low in fat, and high in fiber.

Well-planned vegan diets usually include a wide range of plant foods which provide all of the protein needed each day. There are many plant-based foods which are also considered as complete proteins. So even if you're a vegan, you won't have to suffer from a protein deficiency. In the beginning, if you discover that you're not getting enough protein, all you have to do is increase your protein intake by eating foods such as beans, buckwheat, chia, beans, edamame, tempeh, tofu, hummus, quinoa, lentils, pumpkin seeds, almond butter, and others. Or you can also take supplements or vitamins if that's what you prefer. The bottom line is, just because you're a vegan, this doesn't mean that you're not getting any protein at all. This just isn't true!

Myth #5 Vegans Don't Get Enough Calcium

You can blame this on those cheesy commercials which show celebrities and other people drinking milk with feelings which leaves a milky mustache on their upper lip.

These "Got Milk?" commercials can be so tacky yet so effective at the same time! This makes people believe that vegans don't get enough calcium because we don't drink milk.

But the truth is, just like protein, we can easily get all the calcium we need each day from plant-based food sources. Just like the other minerals, calcium occurs naturally in soil, not in cows' bodies. It's the roots of the plants which absorb the calcium making them very rich calcium sources. By contrast, dairy products aren't direct calcium sources because the cows only consume grains which are fortified with calcium or grass which is rich in calcium. Therefore, it's actually more logical to get your calcium straight from the plant sources. This method is also a lot healthier.

Although dairy products are advertised as rich calcium sources, they also contain high amounts of saturated fats which, ironically, weaken the bones. These fats may also increase your risk of developing certain types of cancers. So, we vegans actually get all the calcium we need from healthy and tasty sources such as chia, tofu, orange juice, kale, collard greens, beans, and so much more.

Chapter 9
Talking to Non-Vegans About Veganism

One huge part of surviving as a vegan is being able to talk to non-vegans without blowing up at them or tearing your hair out in frustration. Okay, so these reactions might seem a *bit* extreme, but there will be times when you'll feel so frustrated that you don't know what else to do. For the most part though, talking to non-vegans will go smoothly, especially if the people you talk to are open-minded or they love you enough to accept your choices.

The ease of talking to non-vegans about veganism depends on the person you are talking to. Despite the fact that more and more people are choosing to become vegans, there's still a good number of people out there who believe the bad reputation which has been around for a long time now. For some of these people, they've had negative experiences or interactions with vegans which is why they have a bad perception of us. For others, they've only heard of these negative comments about vegans, and that's what they have come to believe since. Obviously, these kinds of people are easier to talk to and convince that not all vegans are "pushy or preachy people."

The silver lining you can look forward to is that most non-vegans who have a negative image of vegans generally have the same beliefs and questions. So when you know how to answer these questions or explain why these beliefs aren't true, it becomes easier for you to talk to them. In this chapter, we'll go through the do's and don'ts of talking to the non-vegans around you.

Don't Be Afraid to Enlighten Others!

Now that I've been a vegan for some time now, I find it to be an easy lifestyle to follow. Although I did face a lot of challenges along the way, being a vegan is who I am now, and I'm not afraid to talk about my choice to other people. And neither should you. When it comes to being a vegan, don't be afraid to enlighten others! Notice that I used the term "enlighten." From experience, this is a lot better than preaching or pushing your beliefs on others.

Before I became a vegan, I learned all that I can about it. My journey actually began when one of my friends spoke about being a vegan so passionately. Somebody else had asked her about her lifestyle, and she spoke about it so well that she piqued my interest. At that time though, I didn't ask her for more details. But the thought stuck with me. That's when I decided to learn more about veganism and the rest is history. When I learned all about the animal food industry, I became more and more convinced to try switching to plant-based living.

And when other people ask me about veganism, I gladly enlighten them. That is as long as the situation and timing of the conversation is appropriate. Then if the person I'm talking to just nods and changes the topic, I don't push it any further. But if he or she asks more questions and shows a genuine interest in veganism, that's when I talk about it more. I find this a great way to speak to non-vegans because it doesn't stir strong emotions. From the years I had spent as a vegan, I've learned how to go with the flow, so to speak.

Know Your Audience

So, you've been a vegan for some time now, and you've even attended a few discussions about being a vegan. With all of the new information you have absorbed from different sources, the first thing you want to do is share your learnings to your family, friends, and the people around you. Upon learning that eliminating meat from your diet is beneficial to your health, to the animals, and to the planet, you'd want to spread the awareness to others. Before starting arguments with others about emissions of methane gas, the number of animals killed by the food industry, the amount of water wasted and more, it's important to know your audience first.

Think about what's most important to your audience and start with that. For instance, if you're talking to someone athletic who loves sports and working out, talk about how a plant-based diet provides you with complete proteins which are much healthier than the proteins obtained from animals and animal products. Or if the one you're speaking to loves animals, then you can talk about animal exploitation and abuse which can be avoided by going plant-based. Go back to when you were a non-vegan, but you were already considering veganism. There was probably one specific reason which made you finalize your decision to become vegan, and it was related to your own principles and beliefs. If you want to share the wonders of veganism to others, then you have to know how to approach them about the subject properly.

Keep in mind that going vegan is a very big lifestyle change. In order for one to undertake this change, he or she has to understand WHY it's a change for the better. If the principles behind veganism are aligned with the person's most profound values, then there's a good chance that he or she will be interested in listening to you and in making the change. On the other hand, if you know that the person, you're talking to has a negative perception of vegans, then you must approach the subject more carefully.

When you're talking to non-vegans about why veganism is an excellent diet and lifestyle to follow, learn how to actively listen to the other person too. This will allow you to determine whether the person you're talking to want to know more or if they are just arguing with you for every point that you share. Also, when you're talking to others, never attack them. Doing this is a surefire way to shut down the conversation instantly. Always be kind, be honest, and speak in a polite manner.

Things You Should Do (The Do's)

Often, veganism is a sensitive subject that makes a lot of people feel awkward. Because of this, there are certain ways you must approach the topic so as not to offend anyone or make them feel turned off about the lifestyle and the people who follow it. If you're finding it challenging to speak to non-vegans in general, here are some tips to help you out:

- **Ask questions**

  When you're having a conversation with someone, ask a lot of questions. This is a great way to learn about the person which, in turn, allows you to determine how you will talk to him or her about the matter. You don't have to ask questions which are only related to veganism. Be as creative as you can in steering the conversation, so it doesn't feel like all you want to talk about is going plant-based. By asking questions, you understand others more, and this helps you provide the appropriate answers when they start asking questions too.

- **Affirm or confirm**

If the other person presents a very reasonable argument, give him or her credit for it. Just because the other person objects to everything you're saying, that doesn't mean that you should do this too. Confirmations or affirmations will strengthen your own arguments because it shows that you're open-minded.

- **Don't be afraid to show vulnerability**

Although it's better to spread the good word about veganism, don't be afraid to show your vulnerable side too. It's not a good idea to act as if the whole process was easy for you. This might turn some people off and reinforce the image of vegans as snobs or elitists. That is unless your vegan journey was, in fact, extremely easy. But if you're like me, you would have experienced a couple of bumps along the way. Share these experiences with other people honestly to make you more believable.

When people ask you if you've experienced some difficulties such as cheese cravings, be honest and tell them if you did. To tell your story with all the challenges faced will be way more empowering and aspiring for your audience rather than data dumping them. Once I read this wise thought by Matthew Weiner, it goes like this "*Super confident people with no problems and great marriages and great parenting are not good entertainment.*" In our case

– super confident vegans with no struggles, great health and ethics ate not good entertainment. And to get one to listen, you need to be somehow entertaining in your speech. So, the more honest you are about your own vegan journey struggles and challenges, the higher is the likelihood that other people will take what you're saying to heart. Just because you admit that it was a difficult journey, this doesn't make you any less of a vegan. In fact, it might even make you more inspiring in the eyes of others.

- **Listen actively**

  When the person you're talking to objects to everything you're saying about veganism, don't start getting defensive. Instead, it's time to listen actively and try to reflect on these objections. You might discover that you also had the same thoughts or experiences as that person when you were a non-vegan. In such a case, tell the person that you've been there too. When you show the other person that you're listening actively, and you're not just spurting out vegan arguments for the sake of 'winning the conversation', he or she may see you as less of a "threat" and more of a friend who's trying to share advice.

- **Promote positivity**

  It's all about the positives. If you're speaking to a

non-vegan, focus more on the good side of veganism such as how great you feel, how your energy levels have improved, how veganism helped make you more confident about yourself, and how you've found a new love and passion for food. Talking to non-vegans is different from talking to vegans who are struggling with their own journey. In this case, you may share the struggles you had faced when you started and how you overcame them which is also a positive thing!

- **Share your experiences or stories**

  Have you ever heard the adage, "You can catch more flies with honey?" This is very true even when you're talking to non-vegans about veganism. When you share your good experiences and stories about how becoming a vegan changed your life in wonderful ways, this will make other people more interested in listening. Real life stories are the most compelling ones, especially if you tell them in a casual, relaxed way.

- **Speak casually**

  When you talk too fast or too excitedly, this might make you seem nervous about what you're talking about. So even if it's your first time to speak to non-vegans after becoming a vegan, try to relax and speak casually. Consciously slow your speech down and pause once in a while to emphasize the points you have just shared. Don't think about your conversations as a way to convince others to become vegan as that will really make you feel nervous. Instead, just focus on the person you're talking to and how good it feels to talk to him or her about veganism and about other things.

Things You Should Not Do (The Don'ts)

Knowing how to talk to non-vegans is only half of the story. There are also a couple of things of which you should be aware to avoid so as not to offend other people or give them a negative impression of veganism. To help you become a conversational pro, here are some things you should not do:

- **Never try to start arguments**

  This is one of the worst things you can do when you're talking to meat-eaters. When you reject or make objections to other people's ideas or points of view, it's like you're telling them that what you're saying is better. This definitely won't make them accept or even listen to what you're trying to share.

  When you try to prove that you know more than others, this just affirms the myth that all vegans are self-righteous. No matter how much you've researched, you don't have to start arguing with the person you're talking to. Instead, you should tell them how much you appreciate conversing with you and being honest with you all the way. This shows that you're an open-minded person who accepts what other people say even if these things don't align with your own beliefs. And this is how it should be, everybody is their own person and has the right to decide for himself or herself.

- **Never criticize the person you're talking to**

  Let's be honest, have you ever criticized someone about something they believe in and received a good reaction in return? This rarely happens. Most of the time, when you start your conversation by criticizing or condemning the other person, he or she will mostly do the same thing to you. Soon, your conversation turns sour as you start giving negative responses to one another. As Dale Carnegie says in his book 'How to Win Friends and Influence People' – "... *criticisms are like homing pigeons. They always return home. Let's realize that the person we are going to correct and condemn will probably justify himself or herself and condemn us in return.*"

- **Never judge the business of other people**

  This is very important, especially when talking to people in the animal food industry. For instance, if you're speaking to animal farmers and people in similar businesses, restrain yourself from judgment.

You should never let other people feel bad about how they earn the money that supports themselves and their families. Criticizing such people will make them upset then they'll just get defensive.

- **Don't let your emotions get the best of you**

  This point is a lot easier said than done. Unfortunately, this has happened to the best of us. I have experienced my emotions getting the best of me when I talk to others about topics that I feel very passionate about. Usually, this happens when someone you know makes a mean joke or comment even though he or she already knows your life choices.

  Then you might get angry or emotional then blow up on that person. Of course, he or she would then ask you why did you even become a vegan in the first place if it's too difficult? Oh my God, this question! It starts a whole argument which ends with both of you feeling upset. To avoid this, try to keep your emotions in check at all times. Don't worry; this becomes easier as time goes by. The first part is always the hardest but the more you're able to stand your ground no matter what other people say, the more you'll get used to it.

- **Respond to what the other person says rather than reacting to it**

There will be times when people will try to provoke you by making inappropriate comments or asking you offensive questions. Usually, these are the people who believe the bad reputation of vegans and all the negative myths they've heard about us. In such cases, try not to react to the mean things they say. It's better if you think about what they said or asked and respond respectfully to the other person. For example, if someone asks you something like 'Aren't the plants you eat everyday also suffering?', stay calm and ask back if this person has any proofs that plants actually can feel pain and are sentient beings. I have found out that answering with question can save me a lot of negative emotions. Try this next time you encounter similar question or comment.

- **Don't inconvenience others with your lifestyle**

  We've already established how veganism seems like an alien concept to a lot of people. You may have changed a lot of minds by becoming an excellent conversationalist already. But it doesn't end there. No matter what the situation is, try not to make yourself an inconvenience to others.

  For instance, if you're attending a party, don't force the host to prepare a vegan dish just for you. Or if you're having a potluck, don't require everyone to bring a vegan dish so that you have a lot of options. How would you feel if you're hosting a vegan party and one of the guests says that he or she won't come unless you prepare a non-vegan dish? You'd probably feel bad about this, right? So, try not to make other people feel bad about you, just because you prefer *chili sin carne* rather than *chili con carne*.

Chapter 10
What to Say When Someone Puts You on the Spot

I've said it before, and I'll say it again... a lot of non-vegans find vegans, confrontational, snobbish, and annoying. The sad thing is that it only takes one bad encounter with a vegan for a non-vegan to have a negative image of all vegans in general. Then they start thinking that "all vegans are the same." Therefore, it's important for you to handle all the interactions you have with non-vegans carefully so as not to spread the word of negativism.

Have you ever experienced being put on the spot? While this might not be a big deal to some people, it often makes us feel uncomfortable, upset, and embarrassed. I like to think that when people do that, they do it not because they have a bad intension. In fact, some people genuinely curious and you will have a lot fun enlightening them if you see it this way. I had myself one remembering experience of this kind.

I was meeting with three friends at a coffee shop. Everybody ordered a refreshment and we sat to enjoy the drinks. One of my friends noticed I got a cappuccino with oat milk and she decided to get one herself. She was amazed how delicious it actually tastes and started asking the usual veganism questions. Soon I realize I have been talking about my lifestyle and how great it is for about 15 minutes. This is something I don't advice you to do unless people keep asking you. I was kind volunteering information and I now when I look back, I can see I could have done this in way more subtle manner. Despite the fact I didn't do great in this conversation and kinda 'occupied the scene', I actually achieved something big – I planted the seed in one of my friends. She called me a week or so after that particular talk and told me she did some research herself. She saw two documentaries, read a few studies and BOOM– she decided to go vegetarian for a while and see how this would feel health-wise. It has been more than a year now and she still consumes no meat. I am so proud that I contributed for such a big difference for this one person's life. And even though she didn't choose to go plant-based, I am so so happy that she cut the meat off her diet.

Now, although most people will be supportive, there will also be a few others who will try to annoy you for no good reason at all. This can be extremely frustrating, especially if they manage to ask you a question or say something which throws you off course and renders you speechless. But there are some things you can say to these people without offending them or fueling the pessimistic fire they're trying to light.

9 Most Common Questions Non-Vegans Ask and How to Answer Them

Social situations can be very tricky whether you're a vegan or not. No matter what type of lifestyle you're living or what kind of diet you're following, interacting with others and trying to maintain your composure at all times can be a very difficult task. First of all, you must try to stay calm. None of us are perfect. We all had our own moments where we regretted the things we did or said. But if you want to impress your non-vegan friends to give them something good to talk about, then remaining calm is crucial.

If a person asks you a question, answer it as honestly as you can. Never make up facts or share information which you're not really sure about. If you don't know the answer to the question someone is asking you, then admit that you don't know. This is better than inventing facts which will just lead to confusion.

If someone makes a joke about veganism (and it's not offensive), then try to laugh it off. Laughing along with harmless vegan jokes shows others that you don't take yourself too seriously. Also, if someone is trying to "bait" you to get you to say something offensive back, just shrug it off and move on. Remember that it's always better to be kind rather than confrontational or argumentative. The more kindness you show, the more people will appreciate, accept, and respect you. At the end, veganism is about kindness and compassion, right!

Question #1. "What kind of foods do you eat?"

When somebody asks you this question, don't answer by saying "fruits, veggies, and grains." This response is much too general, and it won't be very encouraging to the people you talk to. Instead, talk about the actual food you eat or the dishes you prepare for your daily meals. This will give others a better idea of what a day of eating vegan actually looks like.

Talk about what food items you substitute for dairy products such as cheese, yogurt, and milk. Or that you eat vegan-friendly versions of common dishes such as meatloaf, Bolognese, and lasagna. You can also talk about your favorite vegan dishes which you love cooking as part of your weekly meal prep. You can even offer to cook a dish for them to give them a taste of what you eat on a daily basis.

Most people are curious about the foods we eat. It's sad that they think that the foods we eat are nothing but fruits, veggies, and grains. Sharing vegan foods with other people is the easiest and most effective way to break down the barriers which prevent people from going trying veganism. So, when the next non-vegan ask you this question, you have a better way of answering it!

Question #2. "Where do you get your protein?"

There are plenty of people out there who act like "the protein police." Obviously, vegans don't drop dead because of the lack of protein. As long as you plan your diet well, you won't become protein-deficient. Still, this is a common question asked by non-vegans.

We all hope that in time, the misconception that protein can only be found in meat and dairy will be cleared up. But right now, this is still a frequently asked question, so you should be able to answer it appropriately. We've already talked about how a lot of plant-based foods are rich in protein. So you can confidently talk about these protein-rich food items which are part of your healthy vegan diet. Again, be as specific as possible by talking about actual dishes you cook, those you order from restaurants, and those which you know for a fact are high in protein.

Most of the time, when people find out that you're a vegan, they turn into nutritionists. They start talking about how we should get all the nutrients our bodies need each day if we want to stay healthy. Also, they might start talking about how the vegan diet doesn't allow you to get all of those nutrients, especially protein. As a vegan, you know that you're getting enough protein so inform them of this fact and of the foods where you get your protein from. This is the simplest way to answer this question. And remember – no eyes-rolling.

Question #3. "If you don't miss meat and dairy, why do you then buy fake meats and dairy substitutes?"

This question can be a bit trickier to answer. In fact, when my brother asked me this question, it made me question myself too. Although to be fair, he asked me this back when I was still starting my quest to becoming a vegan, so I was still in the process of figuring things out.

A lot of non-vegans would ask you why you would swear off meat and dairy only to purchase fake meat products and dairy product substitutes. If you say that you miss meat, then they would ask you why you became a vegan in the first place? When you think about it, this is actually a logical question. But this doesn't mean that there's no good answer to it.

So, when someone presents you with this query, you can start by explaining that like a lot of vegans, you used to be a non-vegan. And you decided to become a vegan not because you didn't like the taste of meat. In fact, most of us used to be cheese addicts and meat lovers. So simply explain that you chose this path because you don't want to hurt animals anymore. Since there are meat substitutes available out there and they're made from plant-based sources, you get to have your burger and eat it too!

Another reason why a lot of vegans eat fake meat, especially at the start, is that they're having a hard time adjusting to their new diet. So in an attempt to stick to veganism, they choose to eat fake meats which taste great but which are made from vegan-friendly ingredients. This is especially true for vegans who have grown up in a totally non-vegan household.

Question #4. "What's wrong with honey?"

Honey is one of the healthiest foods on the planet. It's very popular as a natural remedy too which is why a lot of us probably grew up eating honey frequently. Honey is packed with antioxidants, minerals, vitamins, phenolic compounds, and organic acids. It's affordable, versatile, and oh-so-yummy. So one may ask, "Why can't you eat honey?"

Yes, honey tastes great, and it promotes our health. But just like milk, this is a product that comes from animals; thus, it's not part of our diet. Although some vegans don't have a problem with having small amounts of honey once in a while, the most committed vegans (like me!) have eliminated it from their diet.

Personally, I have stopped eating honey because it comes from bees. These incredible insects play a vital role on our planet. Unfortunately, commercial extraction of honey involves beekeepers taking the honey which the bees have worked so hard to produce only to replace it with a sugar substitute which isn't healthy for them. I read once that one bee needs to work a whole month to produce one teaspoon of honey. Bees need their honey (surprisingly but a fact, they eat it), and if we take it, they cannot thrive. Unlike us, bees NEED honey in order to live healthy lives.

The good news for us vegans is that there are plenty of vegan-friendly alternatives to honey such as maple syrup, date syrup, agave nectar, and more. If you haven't tried any of these, you may want to consider it.

Question #5. "Don't you miss eating burgers?"

If someone asks me this now, I will say 'No, because I get (vegan) burgers whenever I want.' But usually when asking this, people refer to beef burger, which to be honest, at the beginning, I did miss. There's no shame in admitting that you miss burgers, steak, cheese, and other non-vegan food items which you used to enjoy in the past. But after admitting this, remind yourself why you became vegan in the first place. You can also talk about this to the person who asked you the question if you think that it will help make you feel better.

But what can you do when you have a very strong craving for a good burger? When this happens to me, I make a burger for myself. If I'm really hungry, I make a couple of burgers to scarf down all on my own (just thinking of this makes me smile). But instead of using non-vegan ingredients, I use my own healthy vegan ingredients for the patty that I love so much.

If you don't like fake or processed meat, you can use sweet potatoes, beans, chickpeas, and lentils instead. All of these ingredients make for a juicy, healthy, vegan-friendly burger. Go online, and you'll see a lot of vegan burger recipes to whip up from the comfort of your own home.

Question #6. "Can't you at least eat fish? It's the only source of Omega 3."

This is another logical question which you may expect a lot of people to ask you. If you grew up eating fish all your life, eliminating it from your diet can be quite challenging. On the other hand, when you start thinking of fish as animals rather than food, and you start thinking about the pain they go through just to satisfy the appetites of fish lovers out there, then eliminating seafood from your diet becomes easier.

Fish is a healthier type of meat compared to pork, chicken, beef, and others. But it also happens to contain Omega-3. Unfortunately, a lot of commercially-sold fish also contain harmful chemicals such as mercury which may cause more harm than good in our bodies.

There's also the issue of the health of ocean life. Ocean fishing, aquaculture, fish farms, and more, all have a negative impact on our environment. Unfortunately, the more people eat fish, the higher is the demand for it. When this happens, fish industries keep on doing what they do to keep up with the demands.

These are some good reasons why we vegans eliminate fish from our diet. With regard to getting enough Omega-3, we can get this nutrient from plant-based sources such as seaweed, chia, flaxseeds, walnuts, edamame, and more! When it comes to Omega-3 supplements, we all have heard of fish oil capsules and I myself have been taking them for a while before switching to a plant-based diet. What I discovered though is that fish CANNOT make their own DHA and EPA, which are the Omega-3 fatty acids crucial for the healthy structure and function of the brain. Fish can obtain those from algae which they eat. Algae is seaweed rich in those Omega-3 fatty acids and also happens to be abundant in chlorophyll. So how awesome is that! Instead of getting your essential Omega-3 from eating fish that has eaten algae, you can directly consume the algae. Seems like a win-win situation to me – fish get to live, and you get your Omega-3 by shortcutting the process.

Question #7. "But plants have feelings too, right?"

Okay, this question might sound silly (in fact, a lot of people might ask this question just because they're trying to be funny) but there are some people who seriously believe that it's not alright to eat plants because they have feelings too. I'm not joking; some people would ask you why you don't care about innocent cabbages, carrots, and things.

If someone asked you this question in all seriousness, why not ask him or her a question right back? Something along the lines of, "Did you know that around 70% of all land on our planet that's meant for agricultural purposes is devoted to crops which are fed to farm animals? In turn, these animals are processed for animal food products which are in high-demand."

These animals have a consciousness which plants don't have. Also, plants don't have a nervous system or a brain which means that no, they don't have feelings when you compare them to the animals which are tortured and killed to feed the rest of the world. Of course, you should try to explain this to others in the most positive, most polite, and kindest way possible, so you don't end up offending them or seeming self-righteous.

Question #8. "Why are you not skinny?"

Seriously, what person in their right mind would ask you this question? Still, you might encounter some people who (without thinking) might ask you why you don't weigh less when you're following a vegan diet.

Before you react or overreact to this question, remember that most people assume or believe that vegans eat nothing but salads. Therefore, they believe that all vegans *must* be skinny. This is one of the questions which you shouldn't take too seriously no matter how sensitive you are about your weight. Remind yourself that the person isn't trying to offend you, he's just curious why you're not skinny when he or she thinks that you only eat vegetables, fruits, and other foods which promote weight loss.

It's true that following a vegan diet is healthy and it's a great way to cut bad fats from your regular diet. However, this doesn't necessarily mean that you'll lose weight because of it unless this is one of your goals and you're consciously planning your meals for this purpose. But not all vegans lose weight because we're still allowed to eat vegan candy, cookies, cakes, peanut butter, oils, and more. So if someone asks you why you're not skinny, talk about all the fabulous vegan foods you love to eat and how much you enjoy eating them!

Question #9. "Will you raise your kids as vegans too?"

This is one question nobody has asked me yet because I don't have kids. But if you do have children, expect people to ask you this question when they find out that you're a vegan. In most cases, vegan parents are a lot like non-vegan parents. Basically, they want their children to grow up happy and healthy. So if you believe that veganism is the best way to go and you're lucky enough to have found a vegan partner as well, you may want to raise your kids as vegans too. But if you're vegan and your partner isn't, then you may have to talk about it first.

Either way, if you do decide to raise your kids as vegans, you may be doing things a bit differently. For instance, instead of bringing your child to zoos, circuses or other places where they exploit animals, you may bring your little one to homeless shelters or sanctuaries for animals. This shows them how animals must be treated rather than showing them that animals are meant to entertain us.

At the end of the day, it's your decision as a parent to raise your children in the best possible way. But when your child grows up and decides to follow a different diet or lifestyle, be as supportive as you can. Even though you didn't get all the support you needed from your own family when you became a vegan, showing support to your own child makes it easier for him or her to stick with their decision.

Chapter 11
Dating Non-Vegans

Most people who become vegans do so because of profound reasons such as morality. For others, they are more into the diet and health aspect of being a vegan. Either way, becoming a vegan involves making a lifestyle change which requires a lot of planning and consideration. But if you've already made peace with your lifestyle choice, one more challenge you would have to face is dating a non-vegan.

Is there any way for this kind of relationship to work? Where one of you is vegan while the other isn't? The biggest challenge in this situation is that eating together is a staple in any kind of non-platonic relationship. So if you were just beginning your vegan journey, would it be a good idea to date a non-vegan? Or if you've been with someone for some time now, how do you even talk to that person about the lifestyle change you want to make? Should you convince your partner to go vegan too? Or should you just end the relationship for the sake of veganism?

Back when I was still playing the field, there were two main types of guys I encountered when I told them about me being a vegan. The first type were those who felt intrigued about my life choice while the second type were the ones who were just so frustrating to talk to about it. So I either had to talk about veganism throughout the date which got easier the more I talked about it or I had to defend myself to them which, I realize now, I didn't have to! The good news for me is that I found a great guy who accepts me for who I am and what I choose to eat. Thankfully, I don't have to deal with other guys anymore!

Don't get me wrong though, dating wasn't always easy for me, especially in the beginning. Did you notice that I always say that it's tough at the start, but it gets easier? That's because it does. In fact, this is one of the main reasons why I wrote this book. To encourage you and every other would-be vegan to stick with your choice because it will get easier as time goes by.

So anyway, back to dating non-vegans. Just because you're a vegan, you don't have to be in a constant struggle with other people because of your diet and lifestyle. Neither do you have to look for a vegan to date (although this would be a lot easier, right?). There are things you can do to live in harmony with another person even if you don't follow the same diet or have the same principles when it comes to food. And this is what this final chapter is all about.

How to Live in Harmony with a Non-Vegan Spouse or Partner

Being a vegan doesn't mean that you cannot open your heart to another person who doesn't share the same principles and beliefs as you. Getting into a relationship with someone is an exciting, fulfilling, and beautiful experience which has the potential to enrich our lives in wonderful ways. Although it's entirely possible to date or live with a non-vegan, the whole process may come with its own set of obstacles just like any other relationship. When you invest your time and energy in getting to know another person, and you enjoy spending time with him or her, you may want to commit to a relationship. When you find out that this person is a great match for you, love might even blossom. So what should you do when everything falls into place except for the fact that you're a vegan and the other person isn't?

As a vegan, you must follow your own moral compass. If you've made the decision to become a vegan, then it would be best if you stick with that decision no matter what. But if you found someone and your relationship with this person is remarkable in all other aspects, you might be willing to look past the fact that your partner isn't a vegan. There's nothing wrong with this. You don't have to end your relationship just because you can't convince your partner to become a vegan too. If you want your love to grow and your relationship to succeed, this will require a lot of patience and hard work. But as long as both of you are willing to work on the relationship, there's no reason why you can't be together. With that being said, here are some helpful strategies for you to keep in mind.

#1 Establish Policies

When it comes to dating a non-vegan, you must always be communicative and open about what you and your partner should expect of each other. When you think about it, this is true for any relationship too. You must establish your policies and boundaries before allowing things to become more serious. Although some people might feel uncomfortable with establishing policies, this is an important step to take early on, especially if you want your relationship to have a future.

Even before you allow yourself to fall in love with the other person, think about yourself first. This may seem like a selfish thing to say but would you be truly happy with someone when you know that you gave up the lifestyle you strongly believe in just to remain in your relationship? Or even if you don't go back to becoming a non-vegan, how comfortable would you feel if your partner asked you to grab those chicken breasts from the refrigerator while he's cooking in the kitchen? Can you handle non-vegan food at the dining table at each meal? Or can you even handle cooking non-vegan food for the one you love?

This is where your policies come in. If you can handle eating with your non-vegan partner at every meal, but you don't want to cook for him, make this one of your rules. It's important to have a long talk with your partner to state your own limitations and boundaries. Mind you, it doesn't have to be all about you. Ask your partner if he or she or has any rules of his own that he or she wants to put on the table. If you want things to work out, you must learn how to compromise and remain open-minded. And do this from the start so that you know whether the other person is willing to work with you to keep the relationship thriving.

Once you've established these policies, make sure that you stick to them. You should also make sure that your partner sticks to the rules you've set together. If he or she happens to forget anything, don't go on "fight mode" right away. Instead, gently remind him or her of the things you had talked about regarding your dining at home. Remember that nobody is perfect. At one point or another, either one of you might slip up and make mistakes. This is where patience comes in. Keep reminding each other of the reasons why you're together and why you established the rules in the first place.

If you see that some of your policies aren't really working, change them. These rules aren't written in stone. The more you communicate with each other, the stronger your relationship will be. Who knows? When your partner sees how dedicated you are about being a vegan and how enriching this lifestyle is, he or she might even be convinced to become a vegan too! If not, that's okay. As long as you both know your boundaries and the rules of your relationship, you can both be happy and live in harmony with each other.

#2 Get Crazy in the Kitchen

So, you've set the rules of your relationship already. Now it's time for you to introduce vegan dishes to the one you love to show him or her how incredible vegan foods can be. Cooking different types of mouthwatering and nutritious foods for your partner is an excellent way for you to introduce veganism and ease your partner into the vegan lifestyle. Think about the foods you enjoy the most and start with those. Then try getting inspired to whip up new dishes by cookbooks and blog sites.

You can even look for recipes of vegan versions of your partner's favorite dishes too. These days, there are so many resources available which offer amazing recipes which look at taste incredible. If your goal is to convert your partner into veganism, feeding him or her with well-balanced, healthy, scrumptious, and exciting plant-based foods is an excellent strategy. This is a concrete way to share veganism with your partner. Stay positive and show enthusiasm when serving these dishes to your partner too.

After some time, why don't you suggest making dinner your staple vegan meal? If you don't live together, you can agree that if you go out for dinner, you will go to a vegan restaurant. If you live together, you can cook vegan dishes for dinner every day. But for any other meal you have throughout the day, you can enjoy your separate fare.

Another way to incorporate veganism into your partner's

life is by using vegan cooking as the base for his other meals. For instance, if the recipe calls for chicken or beef stock, use vegetable stock instead. Or instead of using heavy cream or milk as one of the ingredients, make use of a cashew cream sauce. There are plenty of vegan-friendly alternatives for the usual non-vegan recipes. Whether you're in charge of cooking or your partner is, you can suggest these substitutions to make both your meals healthier and more vegan-friendly.

Even if, after all of your cooking efforts, your partner still doesn't decide to become a vegan, at least you showed him or her that you don't always have to eat different foods. You can share vegan dishes which you both enjoy. The important thing is that your partner tried the dishes you served and even enjoyed some of them. However, don't make it your life's mission to convert your partner to veganism along with all the other people in your life. If you do this, you might end up being sad and alone. Instead, stick to whipping up delicious dishes every once in a while, without being impatient, preachy or pushy.

#3 Don't Take Anything Personally

As your relationship grows deeper and you keep on trying to convince your partner to no avail, you might feel heartbroken if he or she doesn't choose to follow your dietary lifestyle too. In the darkest days, you might feel yourself getting angry, confused, and bitter because your partner refuses to see things the same way as you. Be very careful though because you might start projecting your feelings to your partner. And this could lead to the demise of the relationship you worked so hard to build.

My final advice to you is not to take anything personally. Each day, remind yourself that your partner just doesn't share your principles or your food preferences. But this doesn't mean that he or she loves you any less. Think about the times when he or she genuinely listened to you when you spoke passionately about veganism. Also, think about all those times he or she tried the vegan dishes you prepared for him or her without hesitation. Or how easily he or she agreed to all of the policies you set for your relationship. Focus on all the good things which have happened in your relationship on those days when you feel negative.

Never guilt your partner whenever he or she orders non-vegan dishes when you're dining together. Neither should you talk about the disturbing information or statistics which convinced you to become a vegan while you're sharing a meal. In doing this, you will create tension between you and your partner which, in turn, might cause a strain in your relationship.

If you want to remain in a relationship with your non-vegan partner and you want your love to grow stronger, keep an open mind and an open heart at all times.

Appreciate every effort he or she shows you in terms of your diet and lifestyle choice. Just because you're in a relationship with someone who eats animal products, that doesn't make you any less of a vegan. In fact, it even verifies your own choice because you didn't end up changing who you are just to make the other person happy. When you don't take things personally, you'll discover that you're a lot happier. And if your partner decides to become a vegan because of you, then that's amazing! But if not, focus on the positives and all the wonderful things the relationship has brought to your life just like veganism.

Conclusion
Embracing the Vegan Lifestyle Without Judgment

Much as we want things to change in our favor, we have to accept that we live in a world where our society revolves around non-vegan food. Because of this, deciding to become a vegan in a non-vegan world can, at times, be very challenging. You'll hear a lot of jokes, a lot of myths, a lot of comments, and a lot of queries which are usually negative in nature being said about veganism. With all the negativity surrounding veganism, a lot of would-be vegans have stopped their quest to follow the vegan lifestyle.

Hopefully, you're not one of these people. I mean, you are just finishing a book entitled "The Vegan Survival Guide" so I'm assuming that you're looking for different ways to keep yourself motivated to stick with your decision. Good for you! Throughout this book, we have talked about strategies and tips you can use to survive as a vegan in this non-vegan world.

One of the most important things to keep in mind is never to become defensive about being vegan. Sometimes you might feel like, as a vegan, it's your personal mission to promote compassion and raise awareness. However, you must keep in mind that not all people are willing to listen. In some cases, you might even end up offending some people when you talk about your own lifestyle which is why you should be very careful and considerate when approaching this subject.

As a vegan, you will encounter different kinds of people and different kinds of situations. While some people are genuinely interested in learning more about veganism, there are some who are just curious which is why they would approach you or ask you questions. You don't have to pretend around the people you love the most nor should you hide your beliefs just to satisfy those around you. The key is to be as low-key as possible while still remaining open to those who speak to you about your lifestyle.

If you have made the choice to go vegan, embrace it! Just don't try to convince other people to become vegans too, especially when it's neither the time nor place to do so. If you remain open-minded and you don't take anything personally, you will be able to stick to your choice without causing negativity to you or others. Whether you're a beginner or you've been a vegan for some time now, everything we've gone through from chapter one to chapter eleven can help you not just survive but thrive as a vegan. So keep your head up and keep on going. And cheers to you, me, and everyone else who has decided to live their healthiest life!

Made in the USA
Monee, IL
03 February 2020